# THE INVISIBLE YOKE
Volume IV

MATT EICH

# We, the Free

STURM & DRANG

*To my fellow Americans,
may we live by love, not fear*

**A New National Anthem**

Ada Limón

The truth is, I've never cared for the National
Anthem. If you think about it, it's not a good
song. Too high for most of us with "the rockets
red glare" and then there are the bombs.
(Always, always, there is war and bombs.)
Once, I sang it at homecoming and threw
even the tenacious high school band off key.
But the song didn't mean anything, just a call
to the field, something to get through before
the pummeling of youth. And what of the stanzas
we never sing, the third that mentions "no refuge
could save the hireling and the slave"? Perhaps,
the truth is, every song of this country
has an unsung third stanza, something brutal
snaking underneath us as we blindly sing
the high notes with a beer sloshing in the stands
hoping our team wins. Don't get me wrong, I do
like the flag, how it undulates in the wind
like water, elemental, and best when it's humbled,
brought to its knees, clung to by someone who
has lost everything, when it's not a weapon,
when it flickers, when it folds up so perfectly
you can keep it until it's needed, until you can
love it again, until the song in your mouth feels
like sustenance, a song where the notes are sung
by even the ageless woods, the short-grass plains,
the Red River Gorge, the fistful of land left
unpoisoned, that song that's our birthright,
that's sung in silence when it's too hard to go on,
that sounds like someone's rough fingers weaving
into another's, that sounds like a match being lit
in an endless cave, the song that says my bones
are your bones, and your bones are my bones,
and isn't that enough?

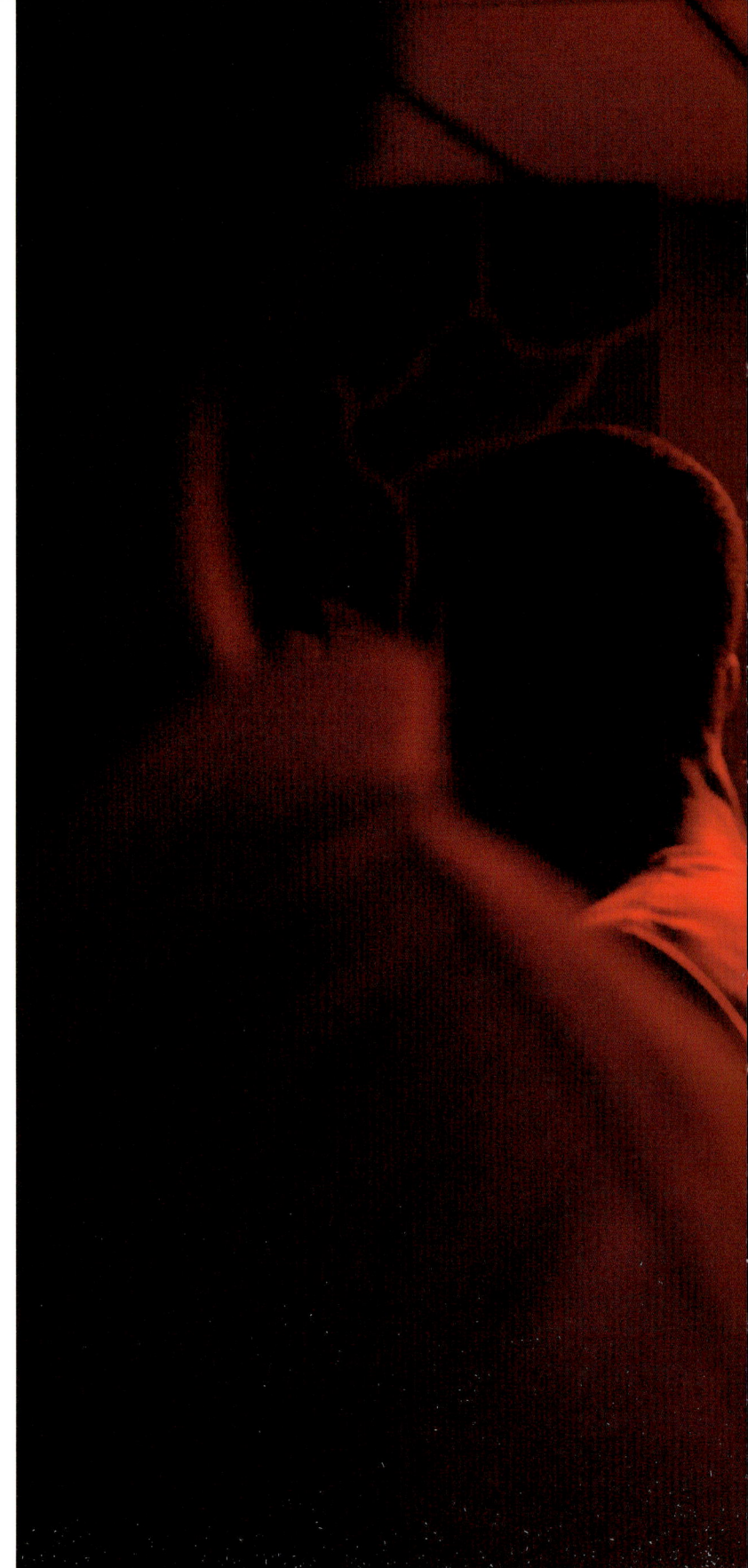

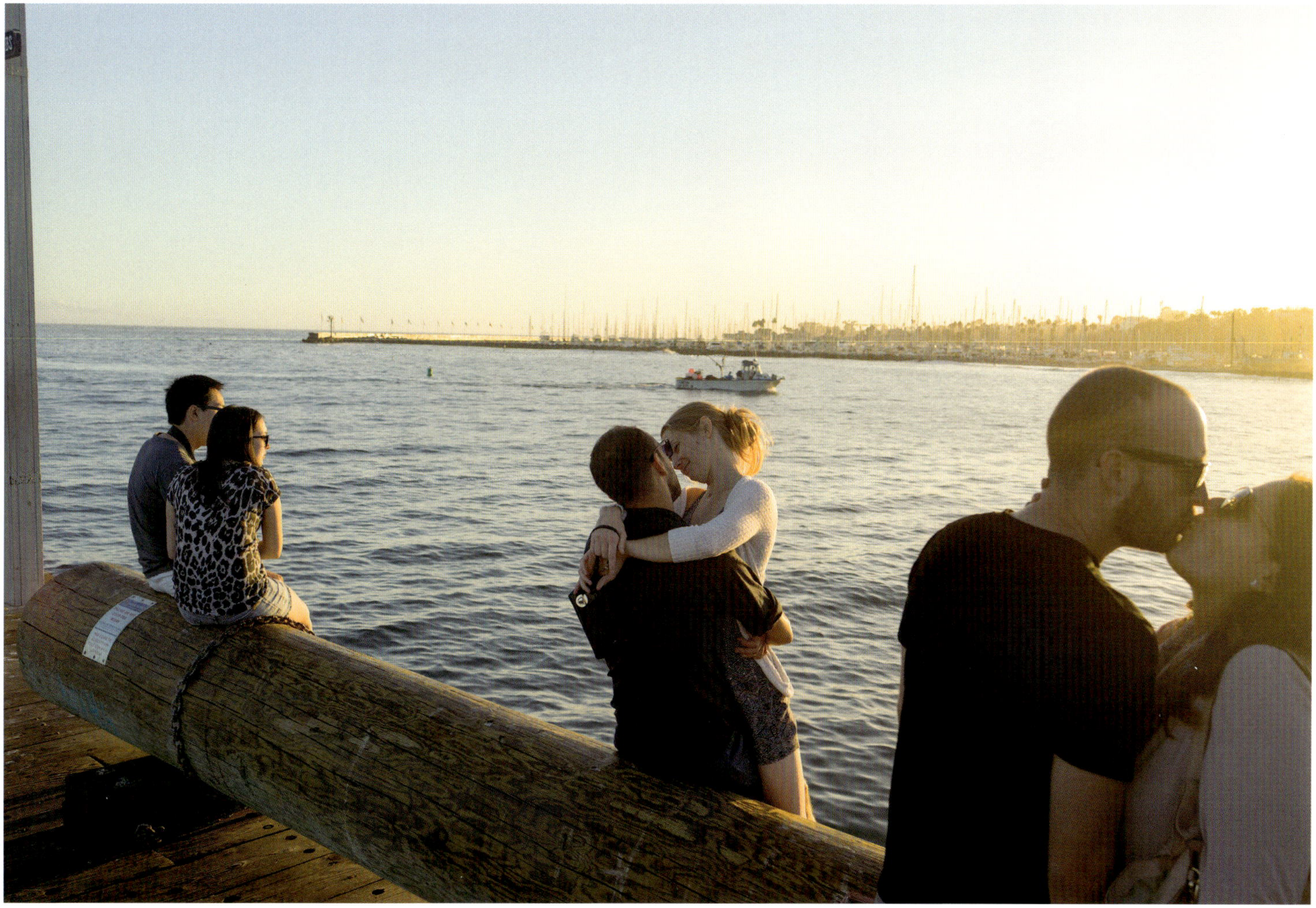

R8
Priority Seating
for persons with disabilities
Fix&Fortify
Improving. non-stop.

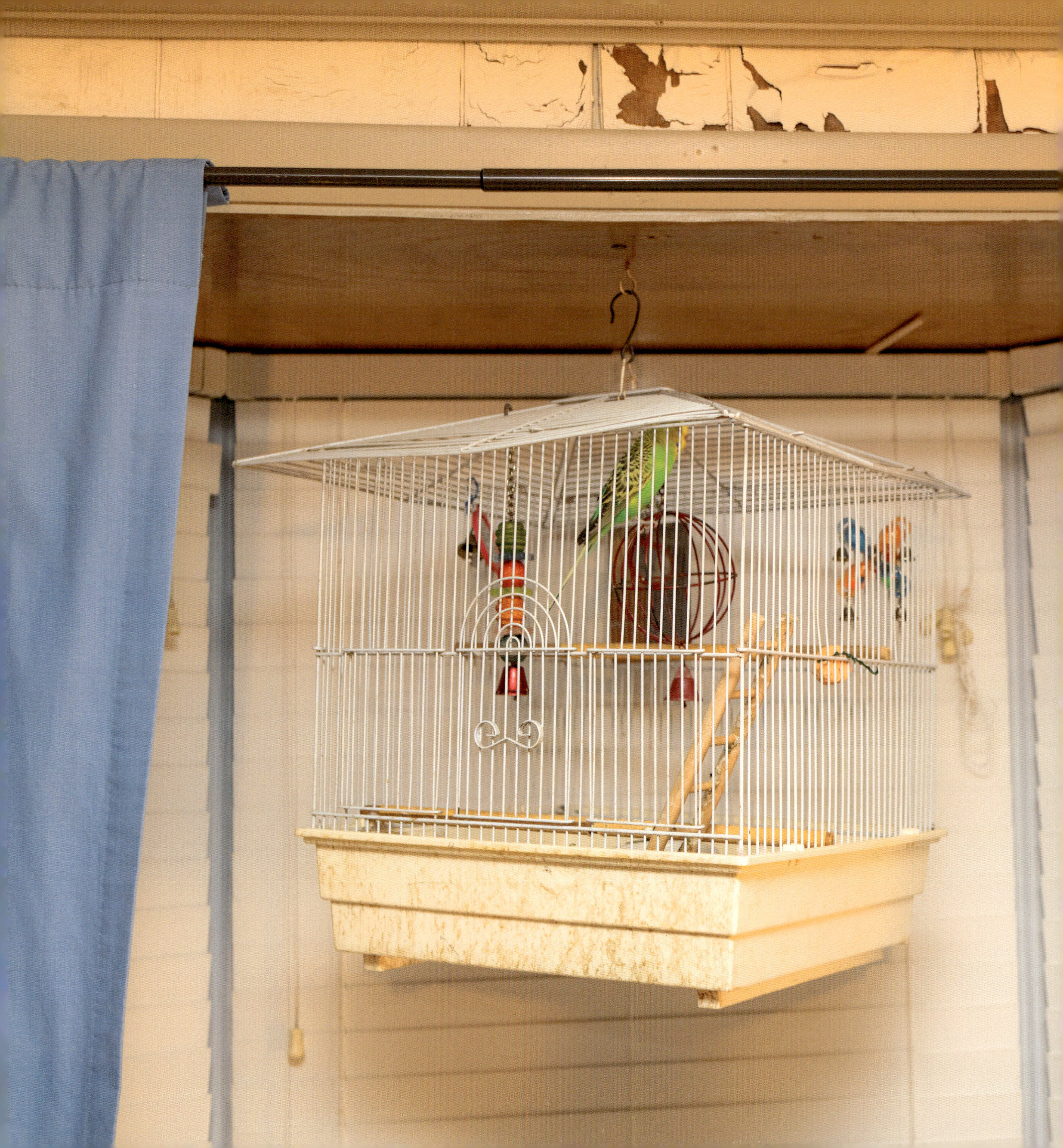

39

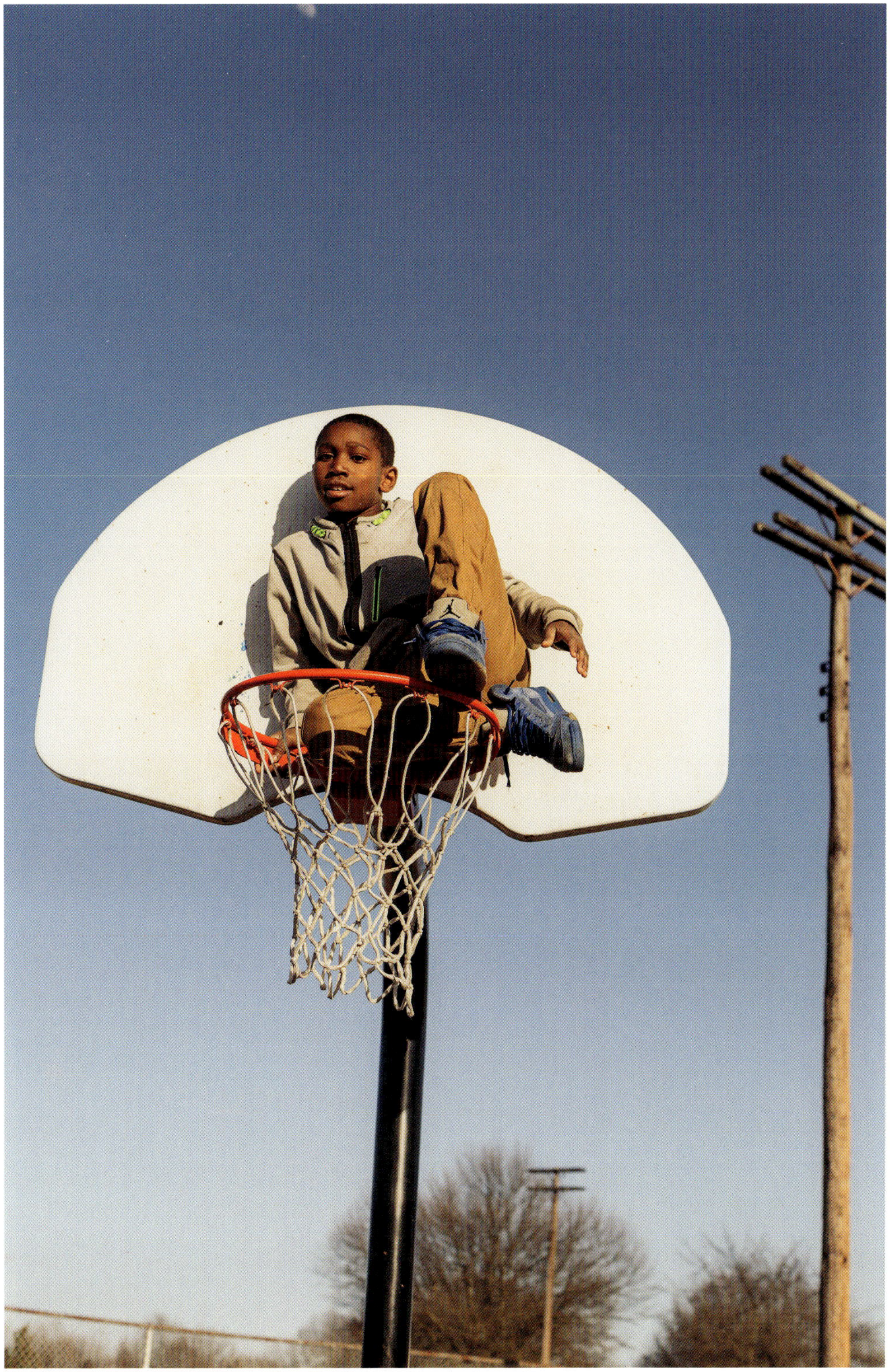

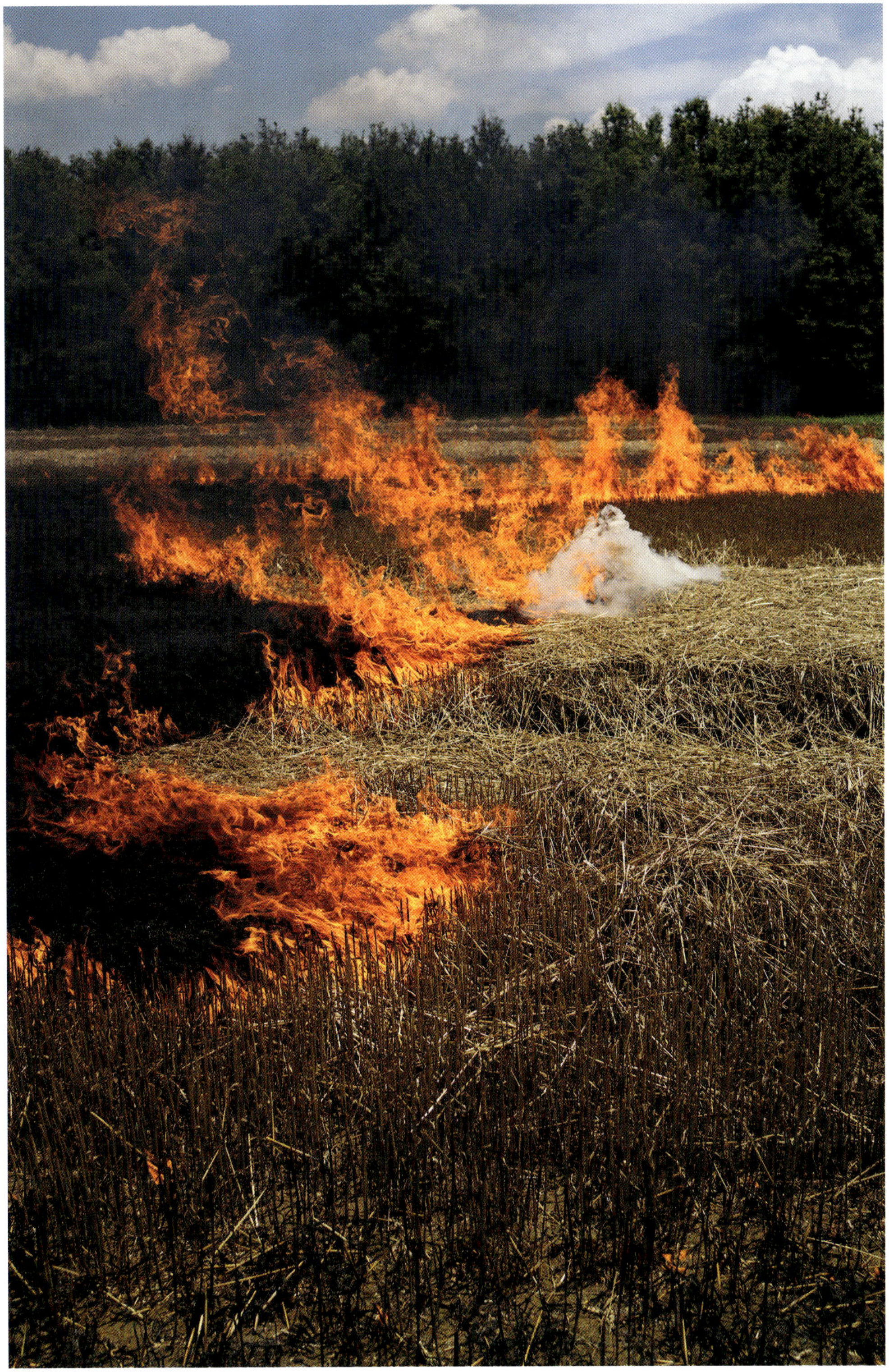

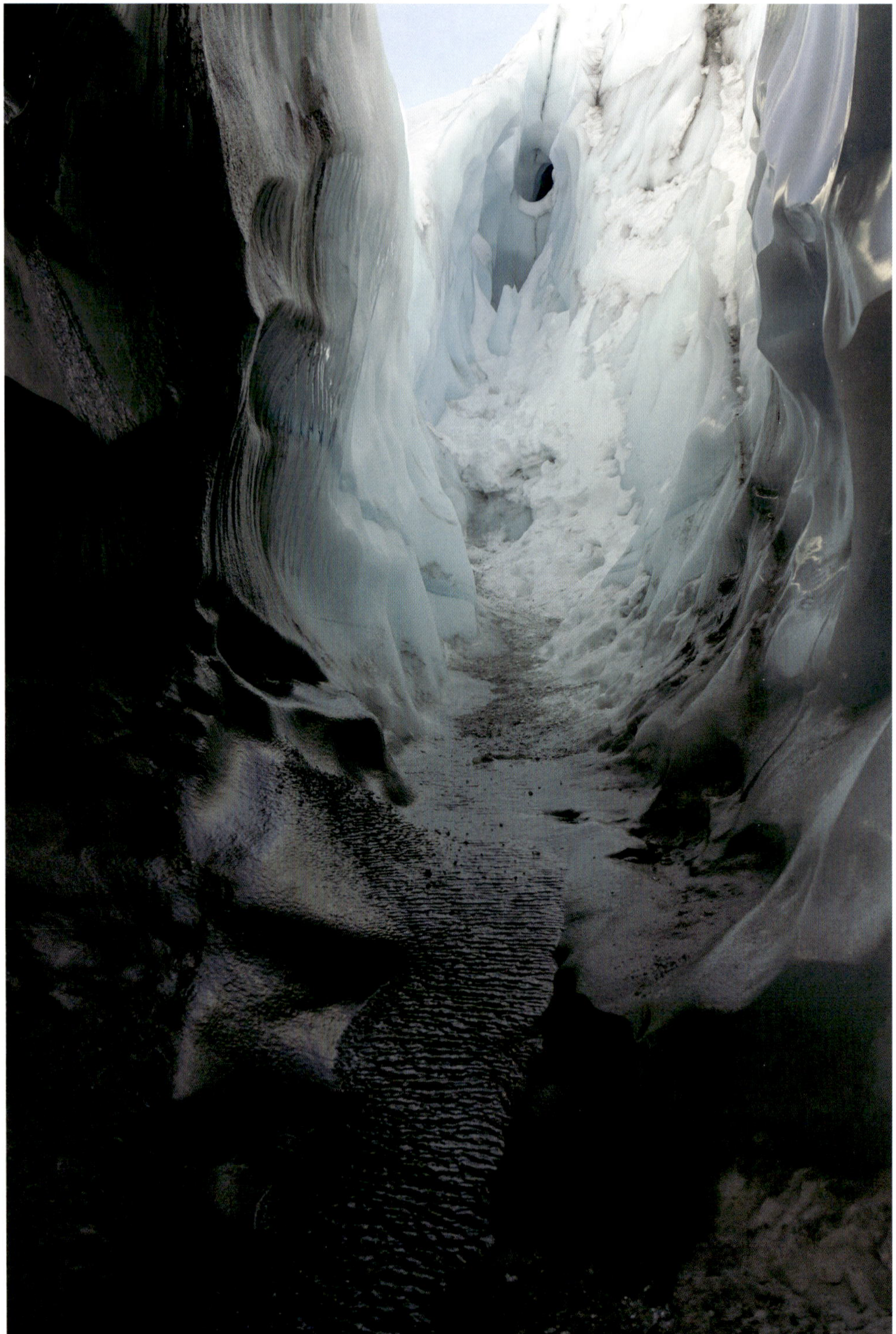

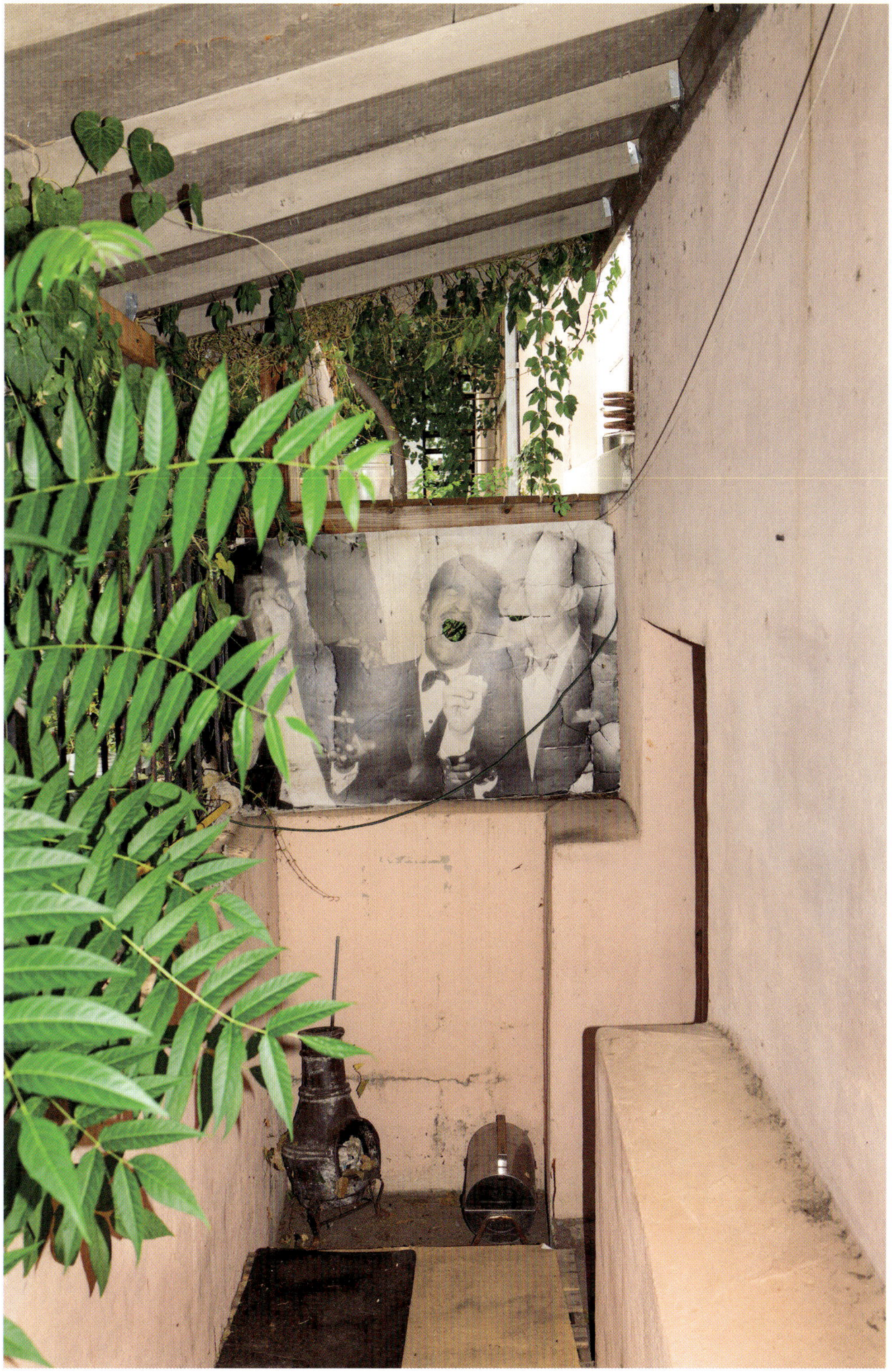

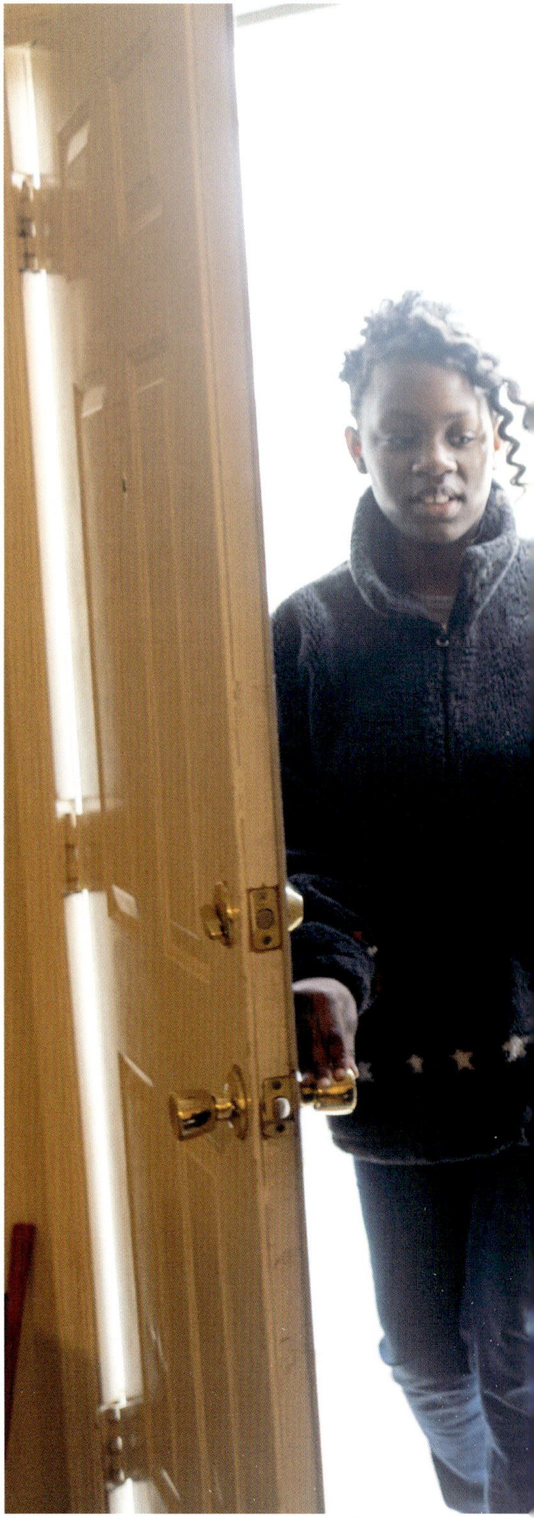

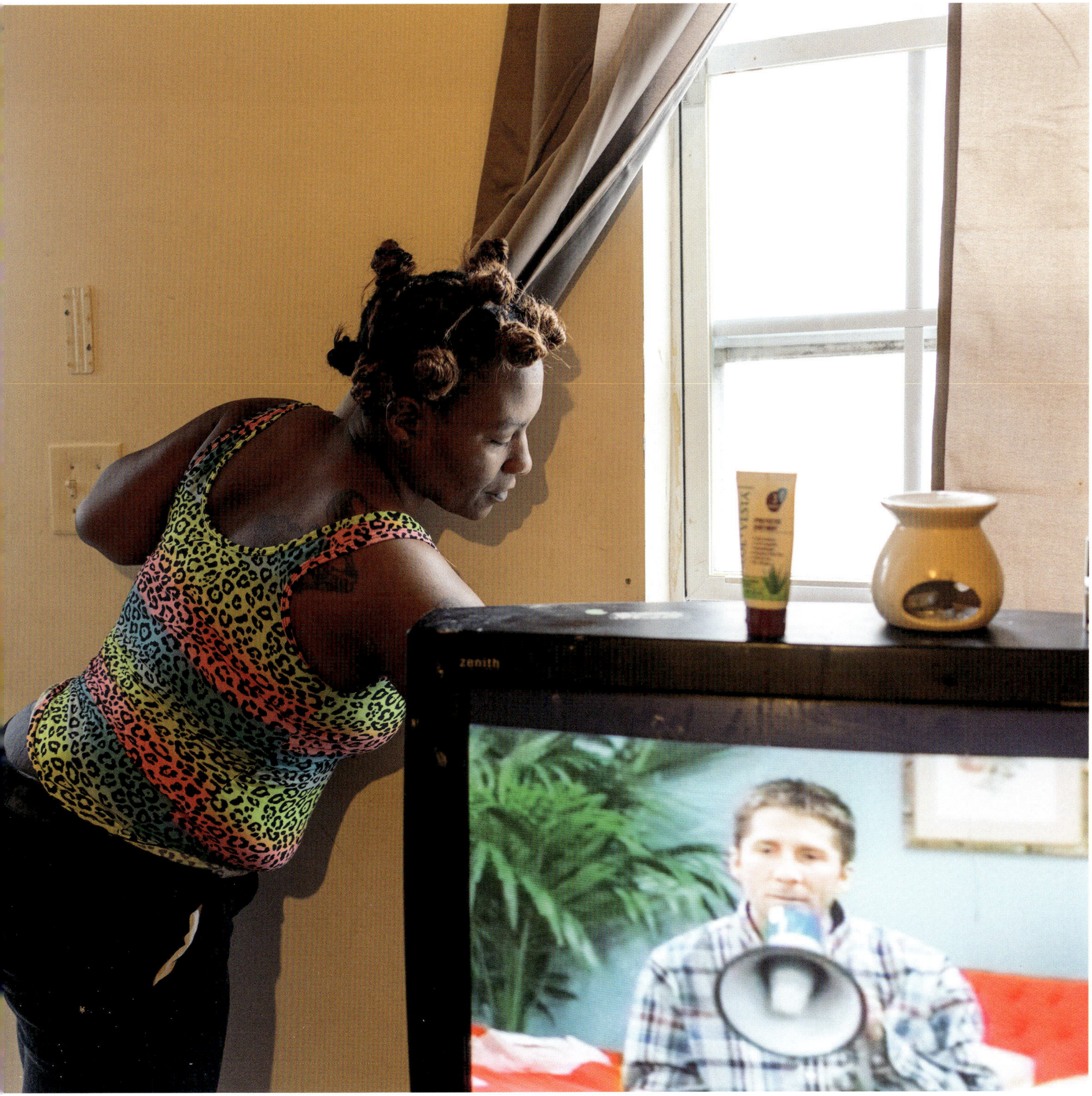
zenith

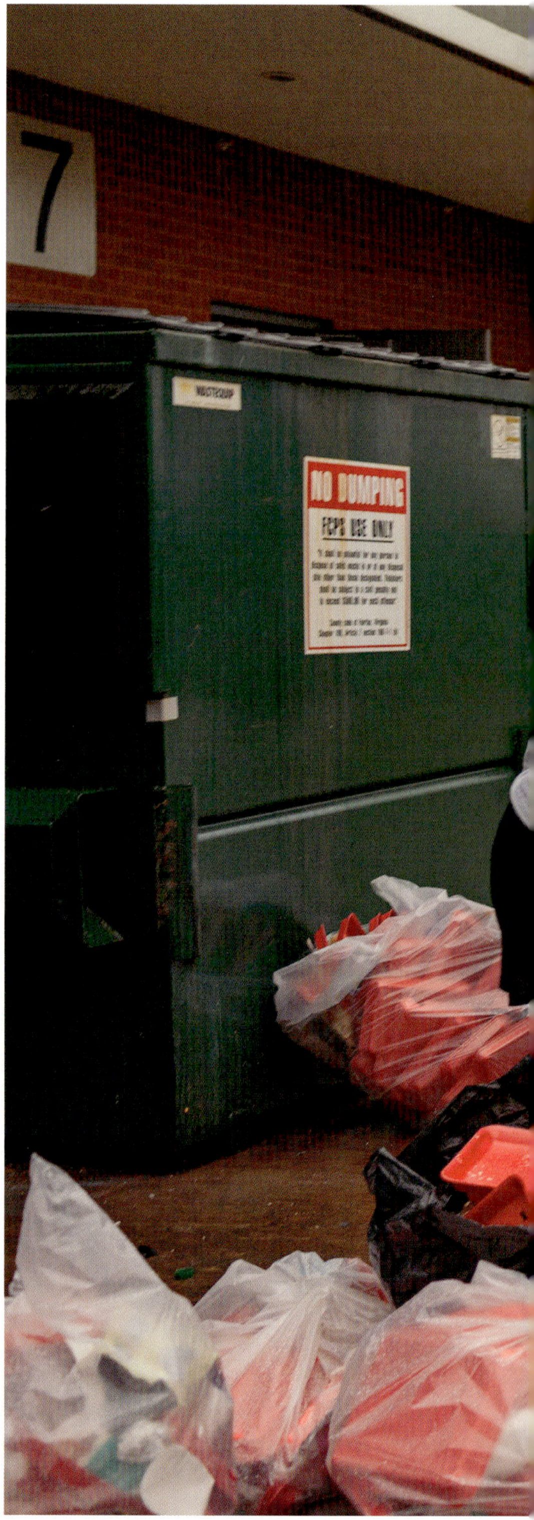
NO DUMPING
FCPS USE ONLY

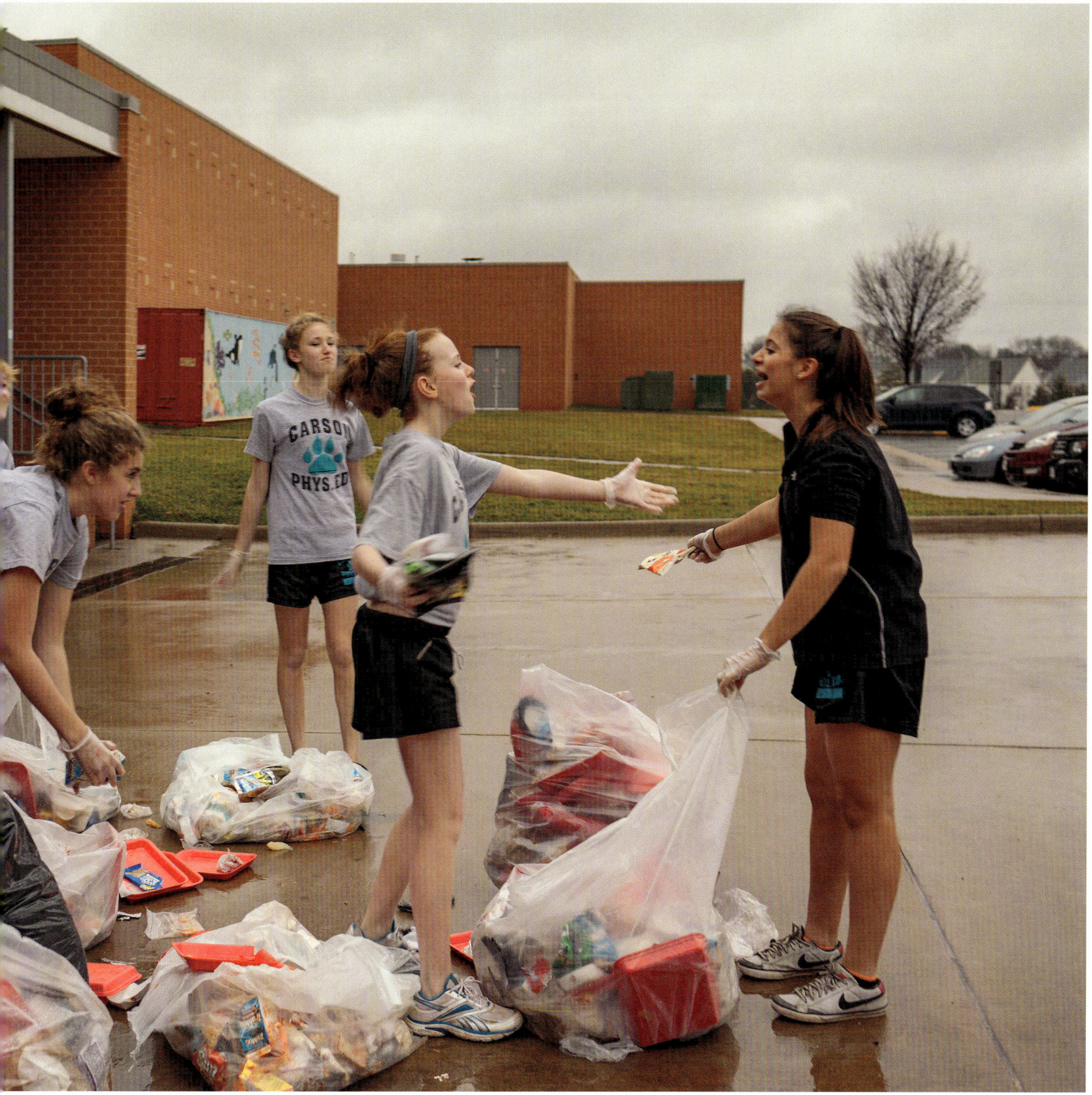
CARSON
PHYS.ED

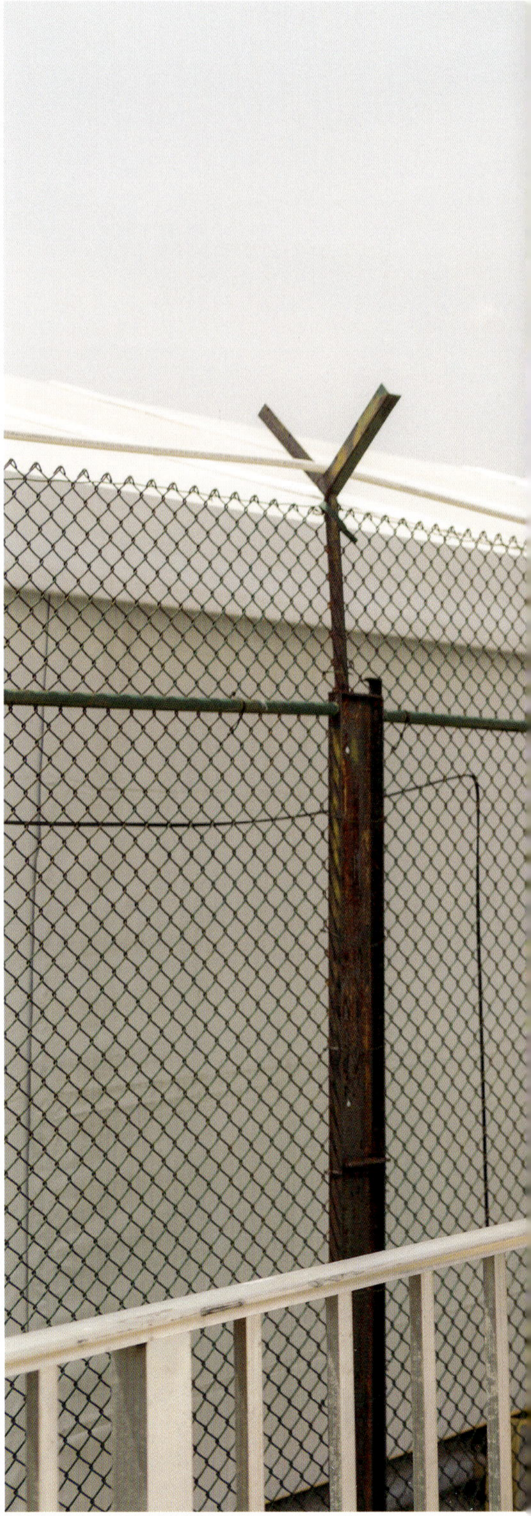

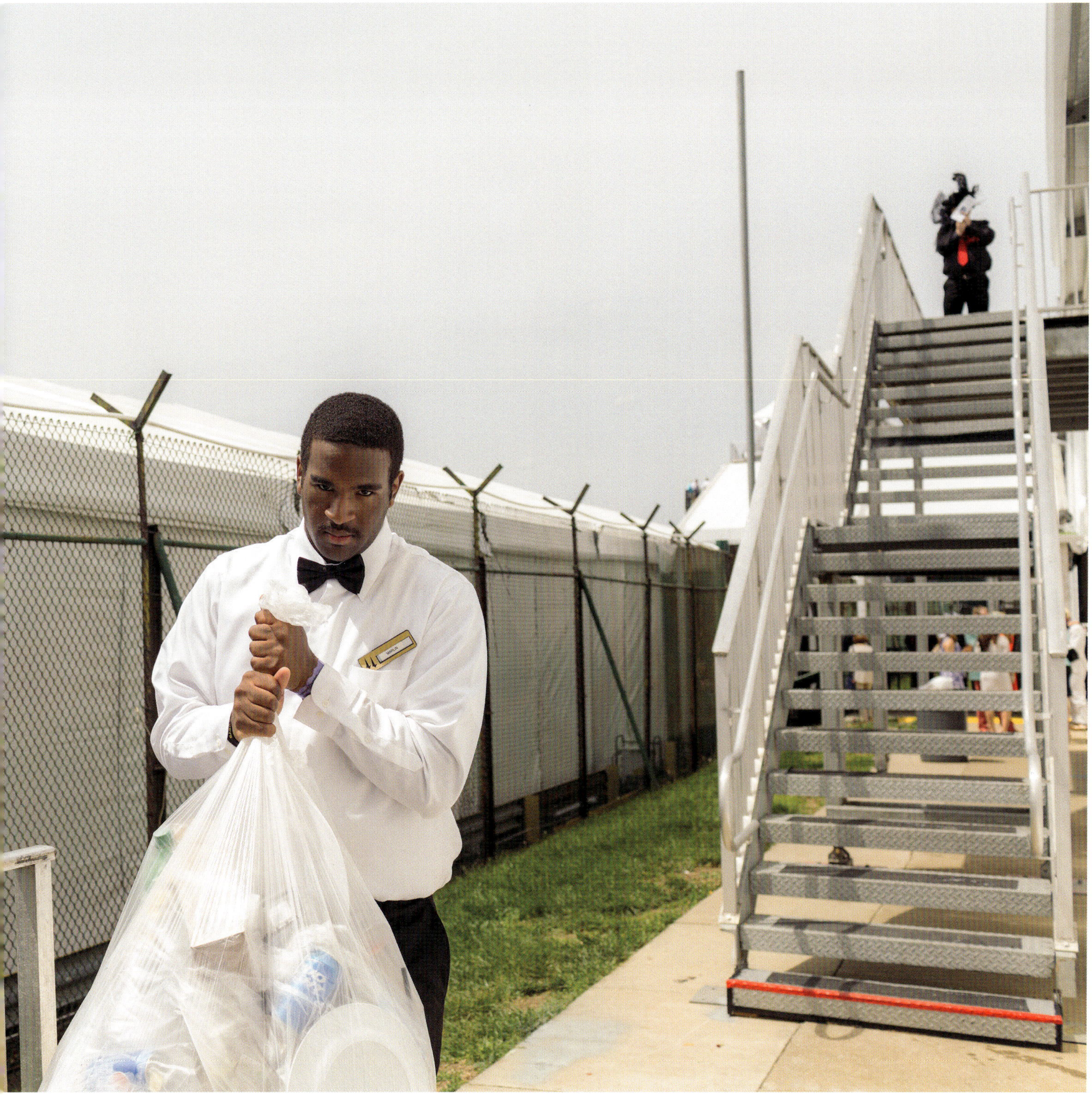

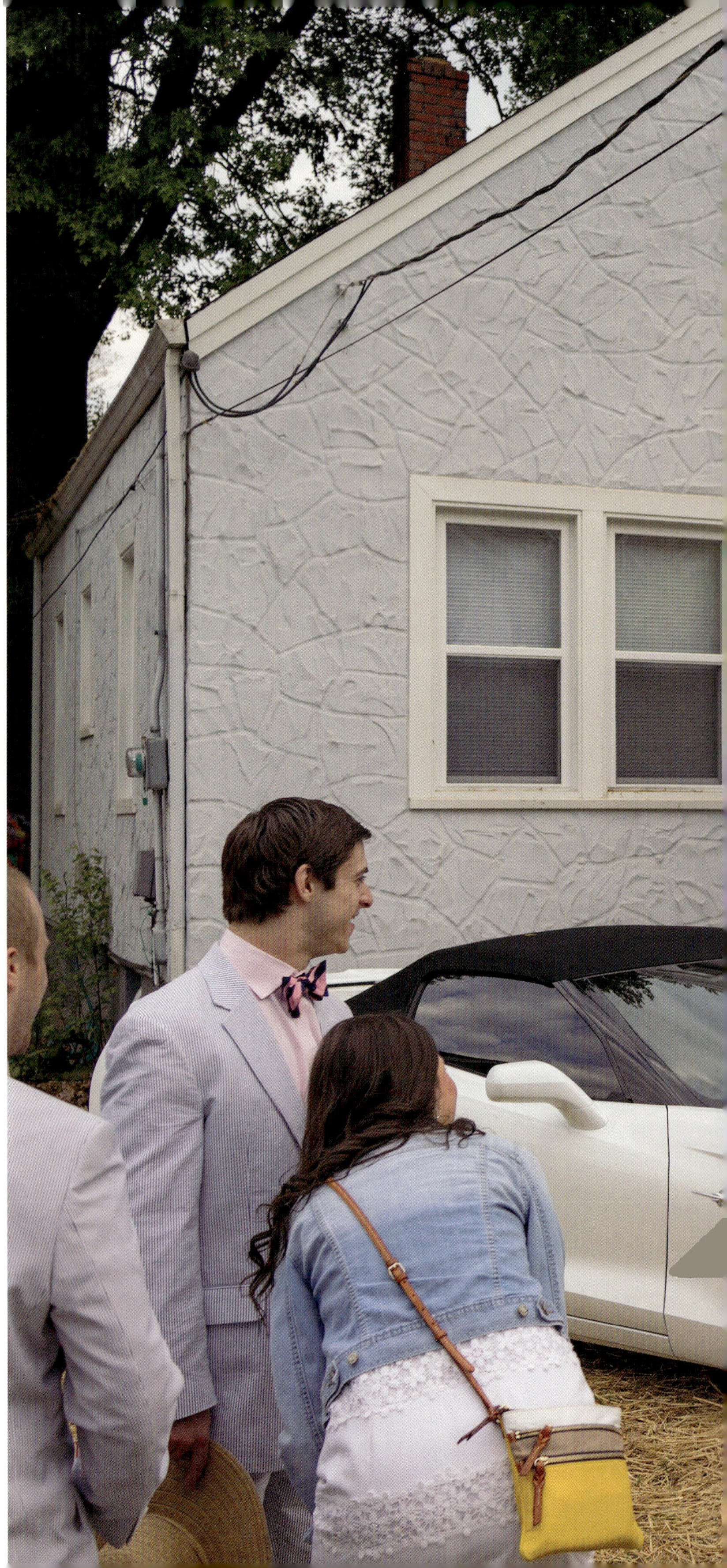

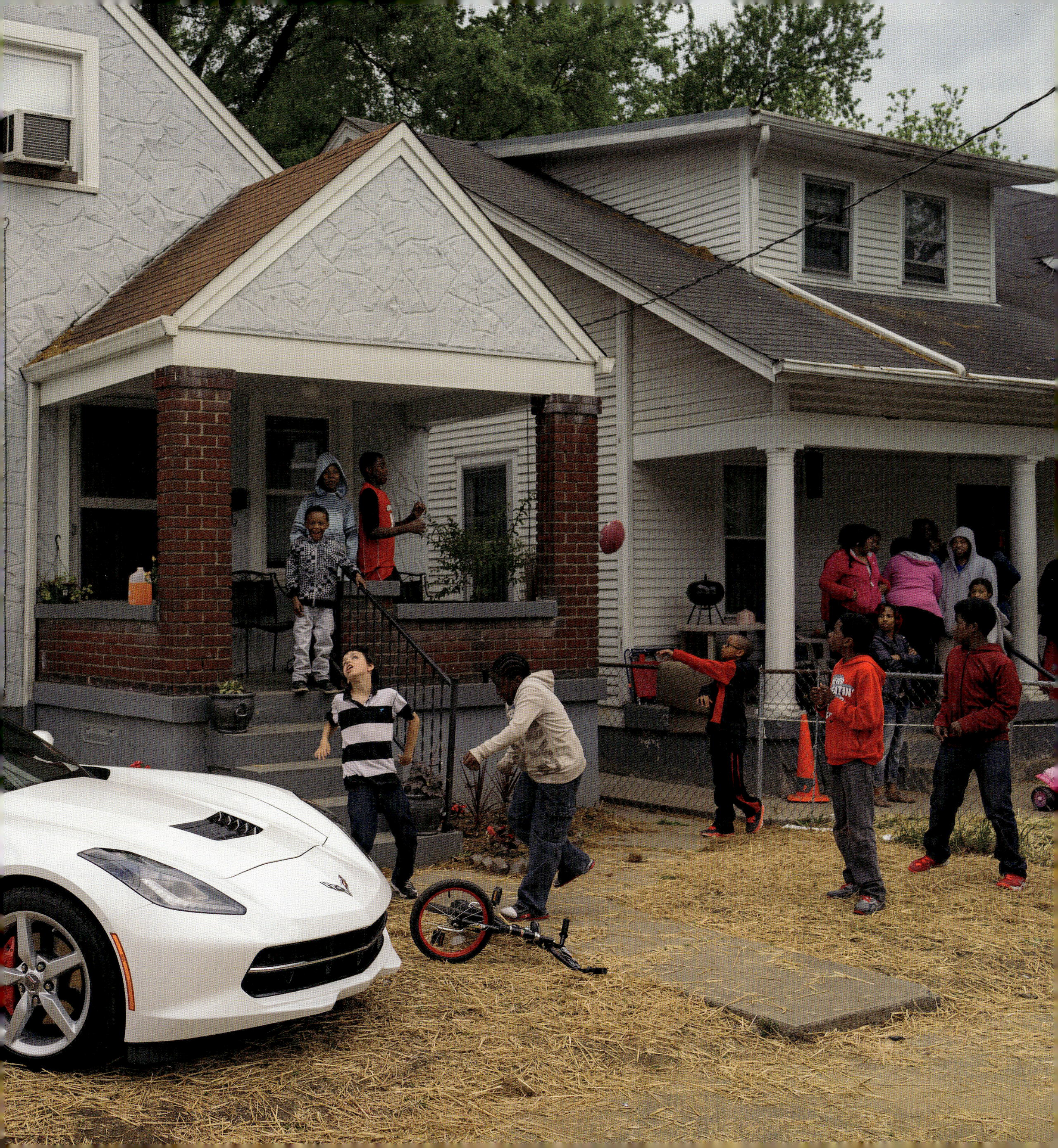

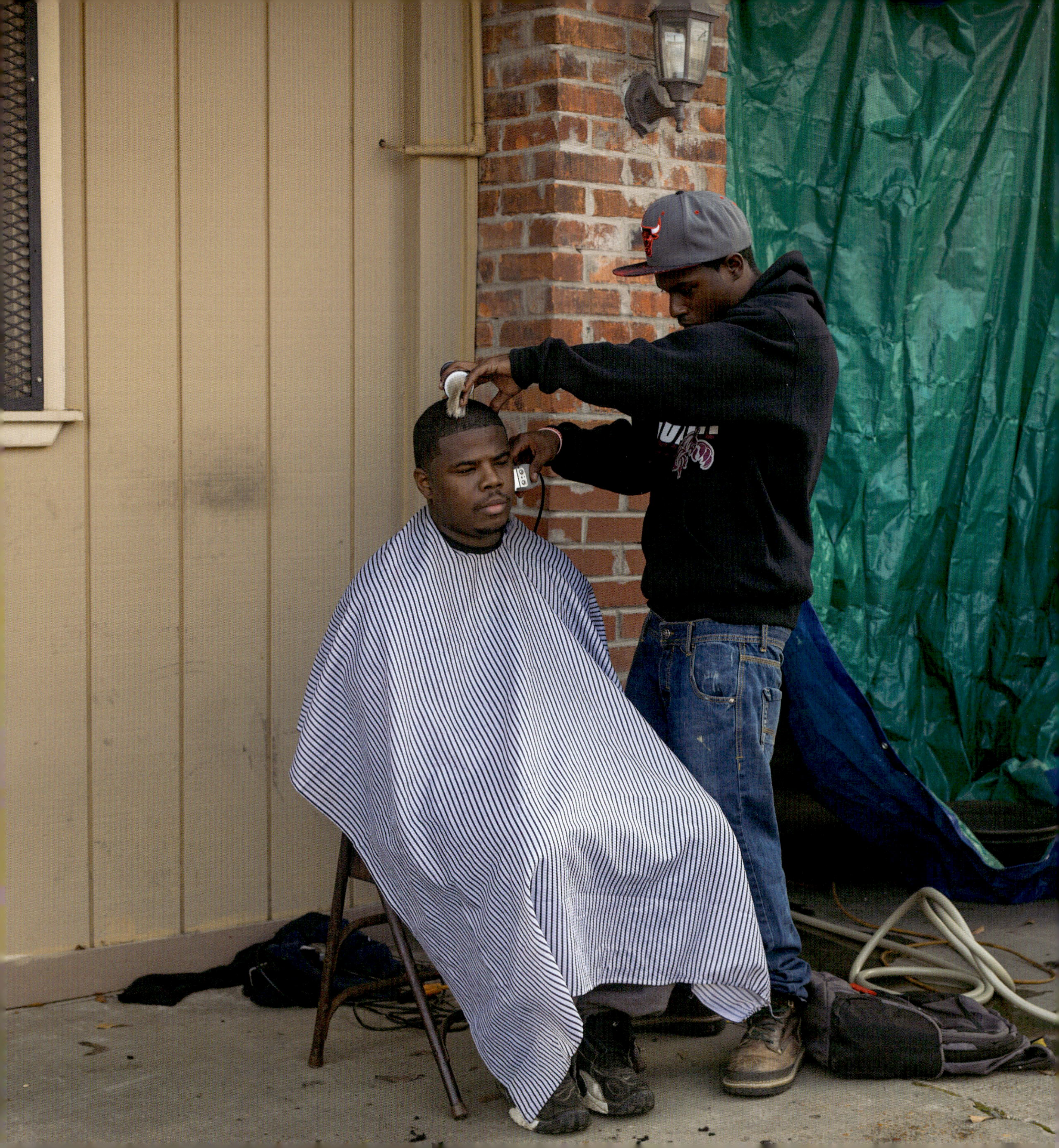

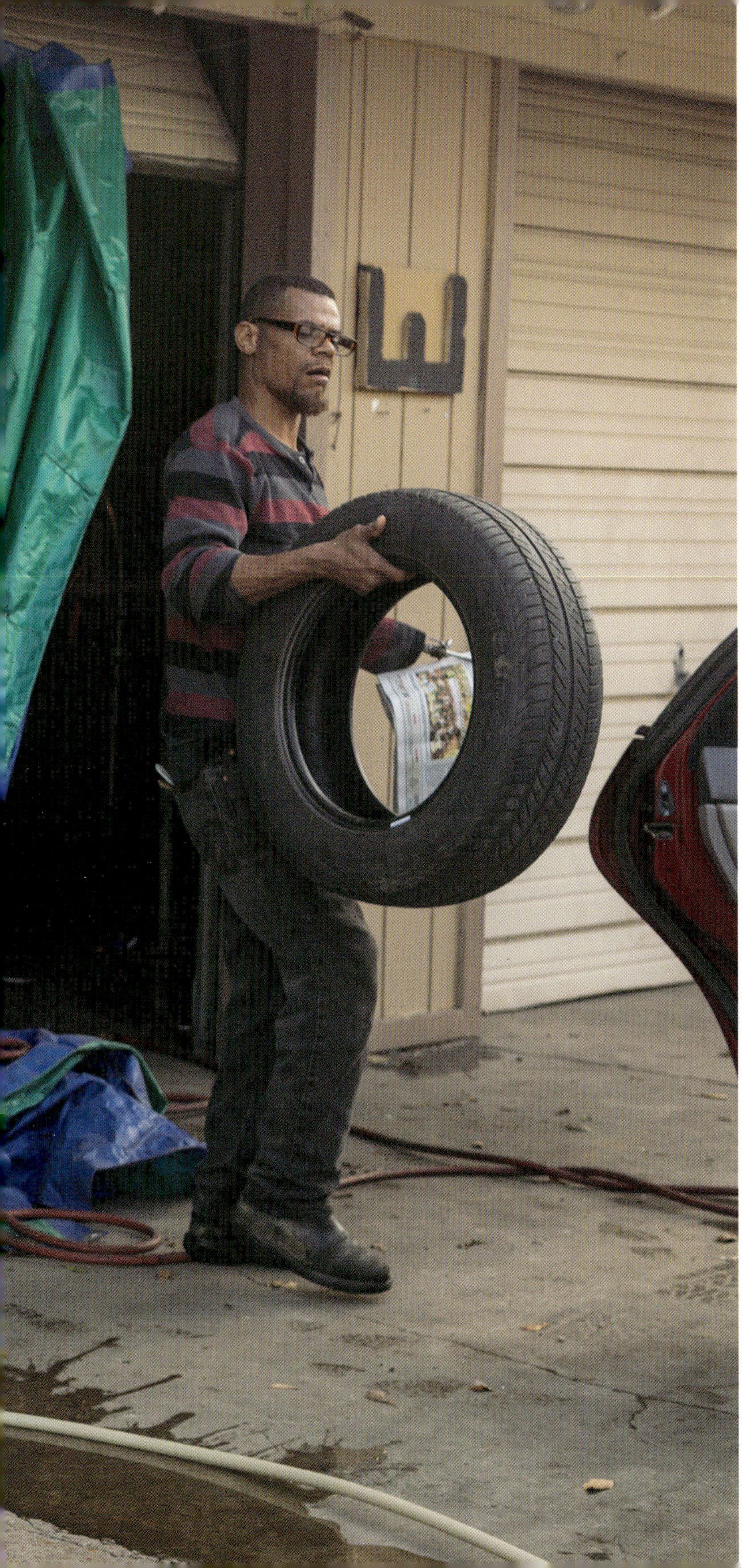

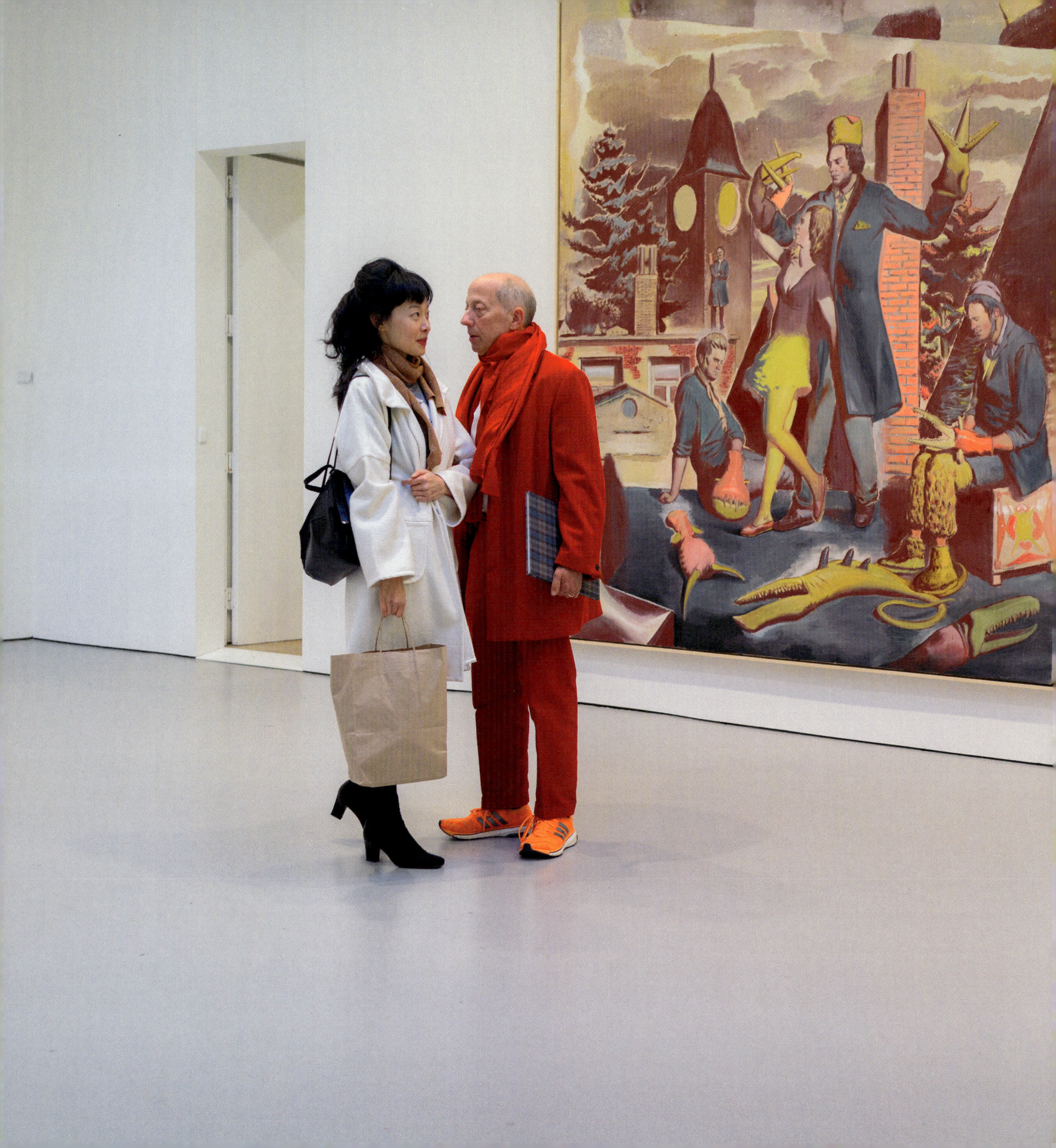

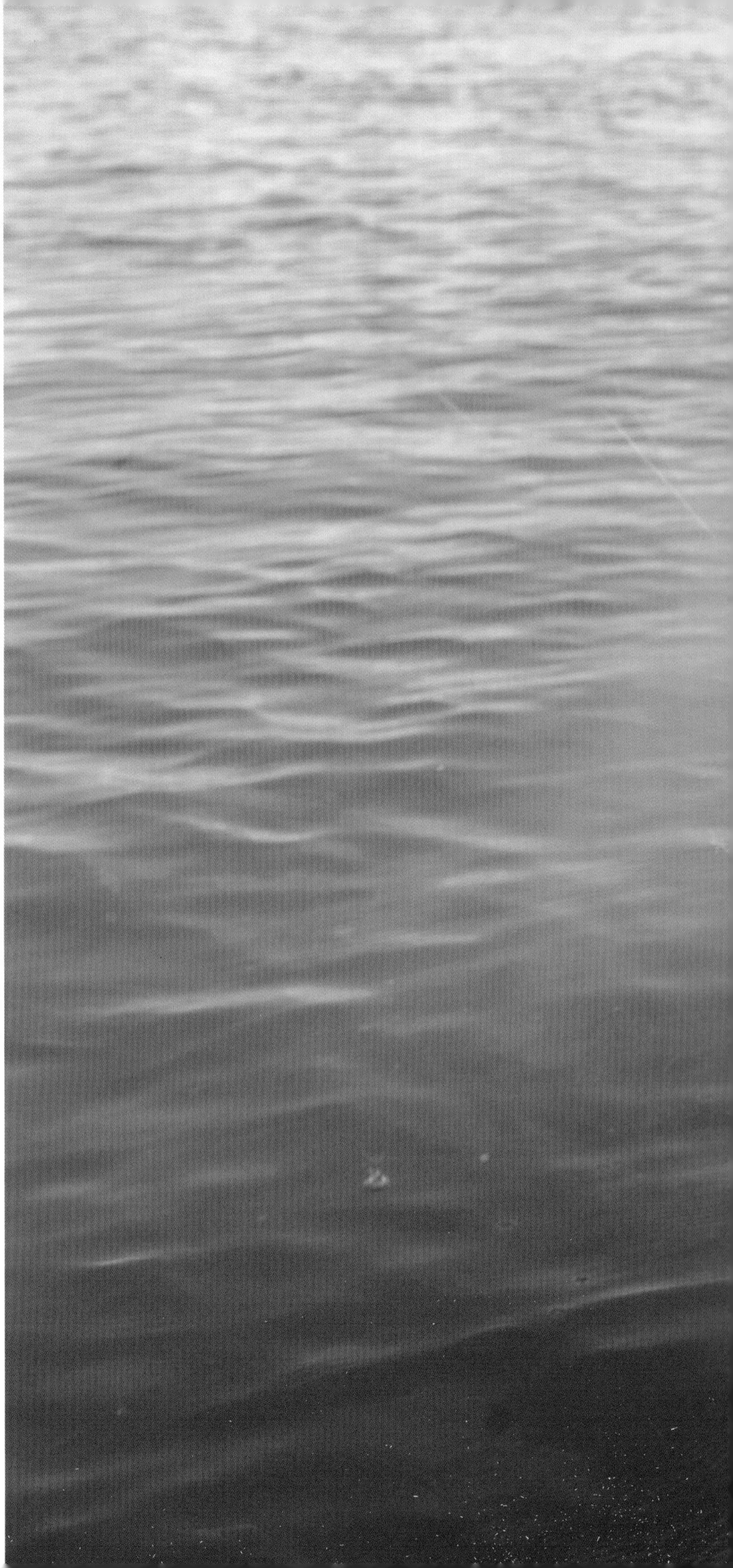

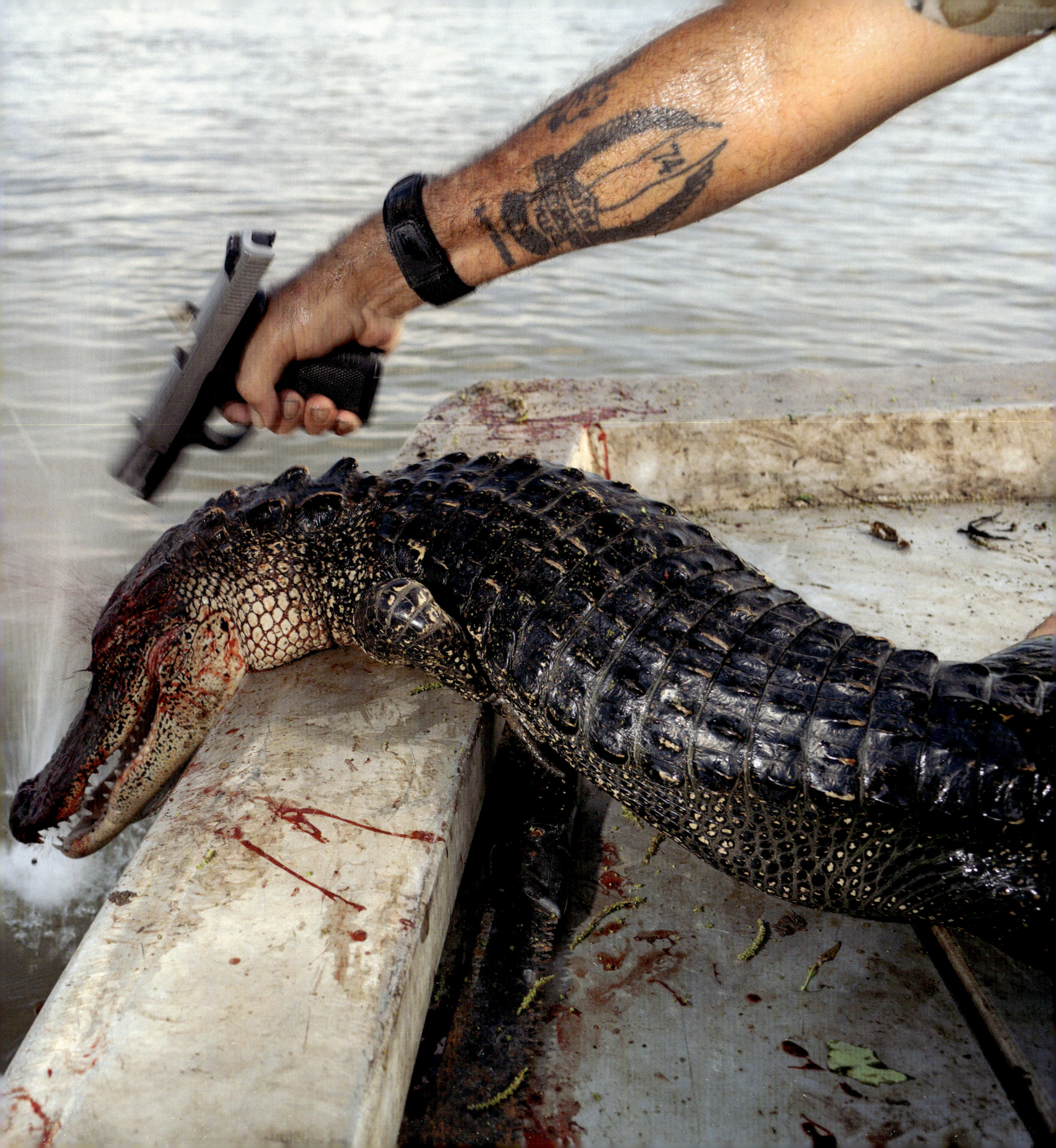

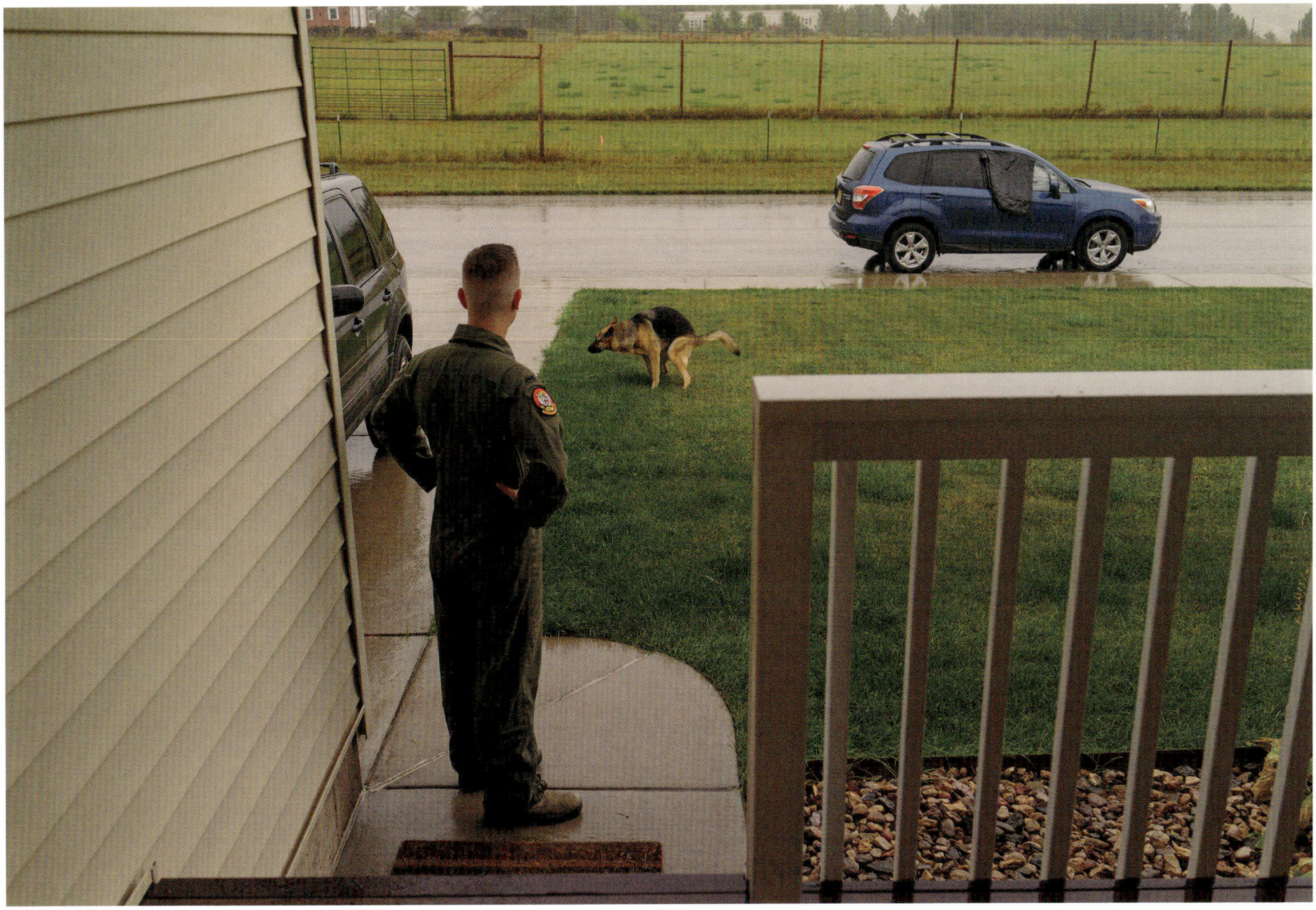

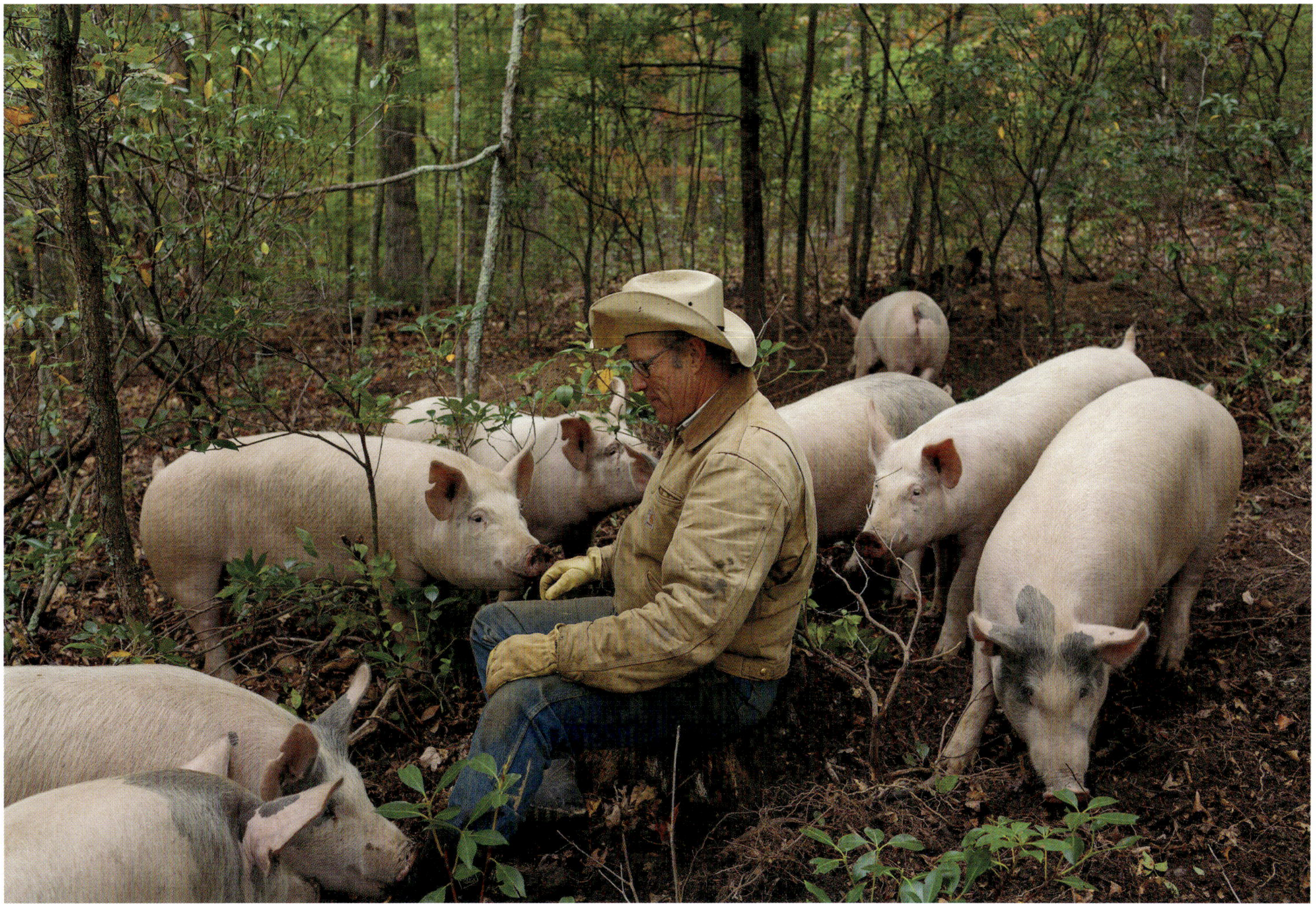

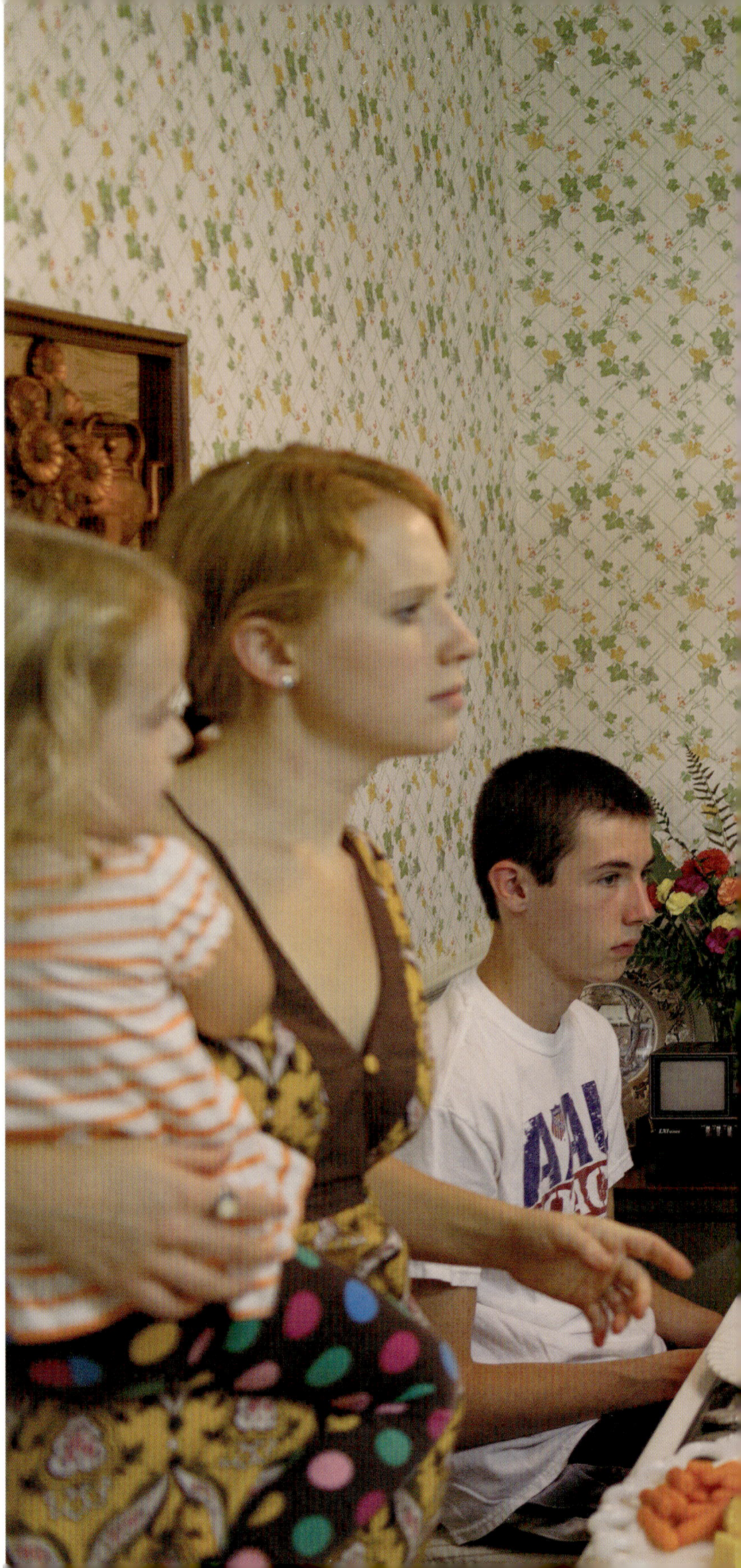

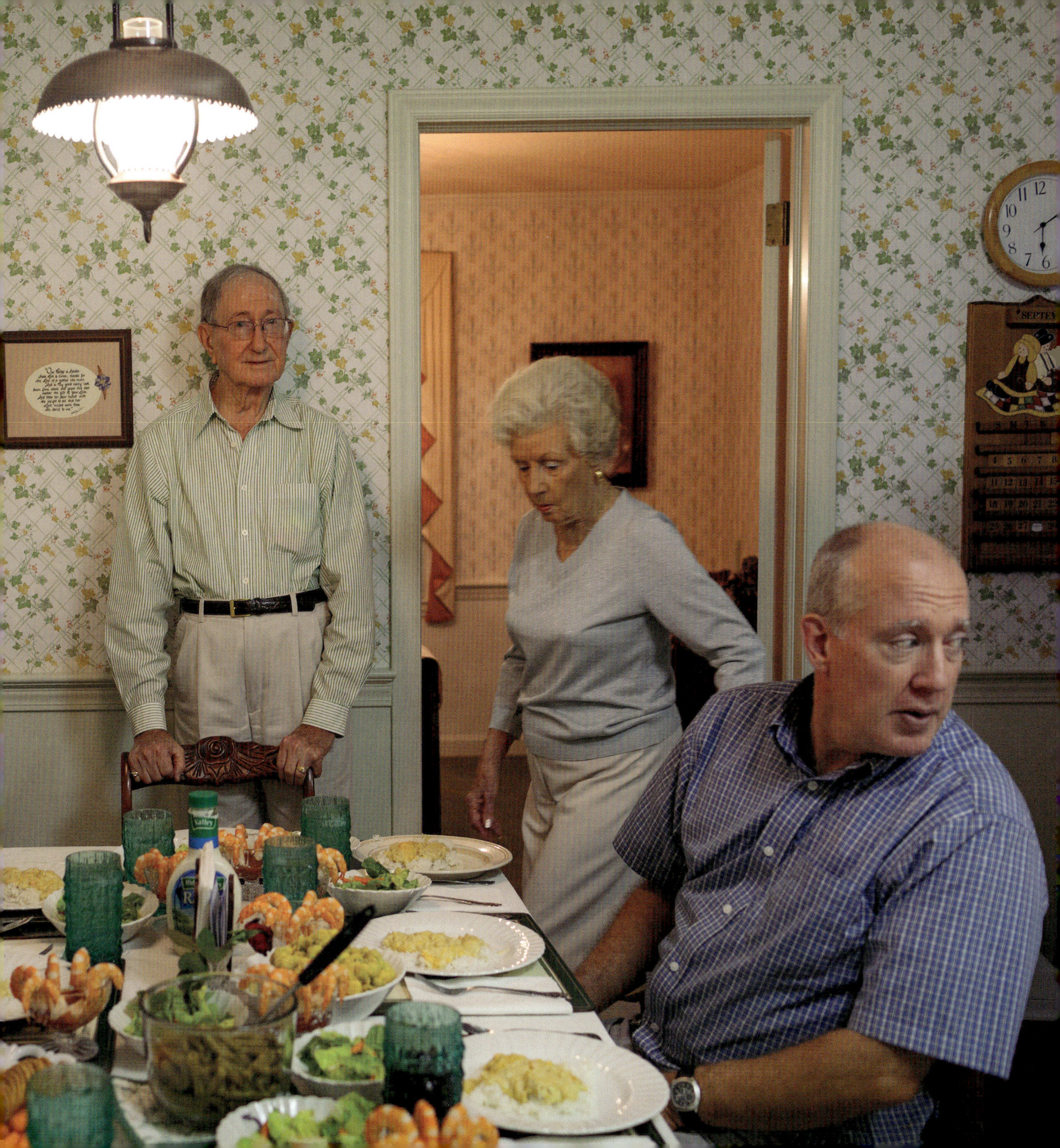

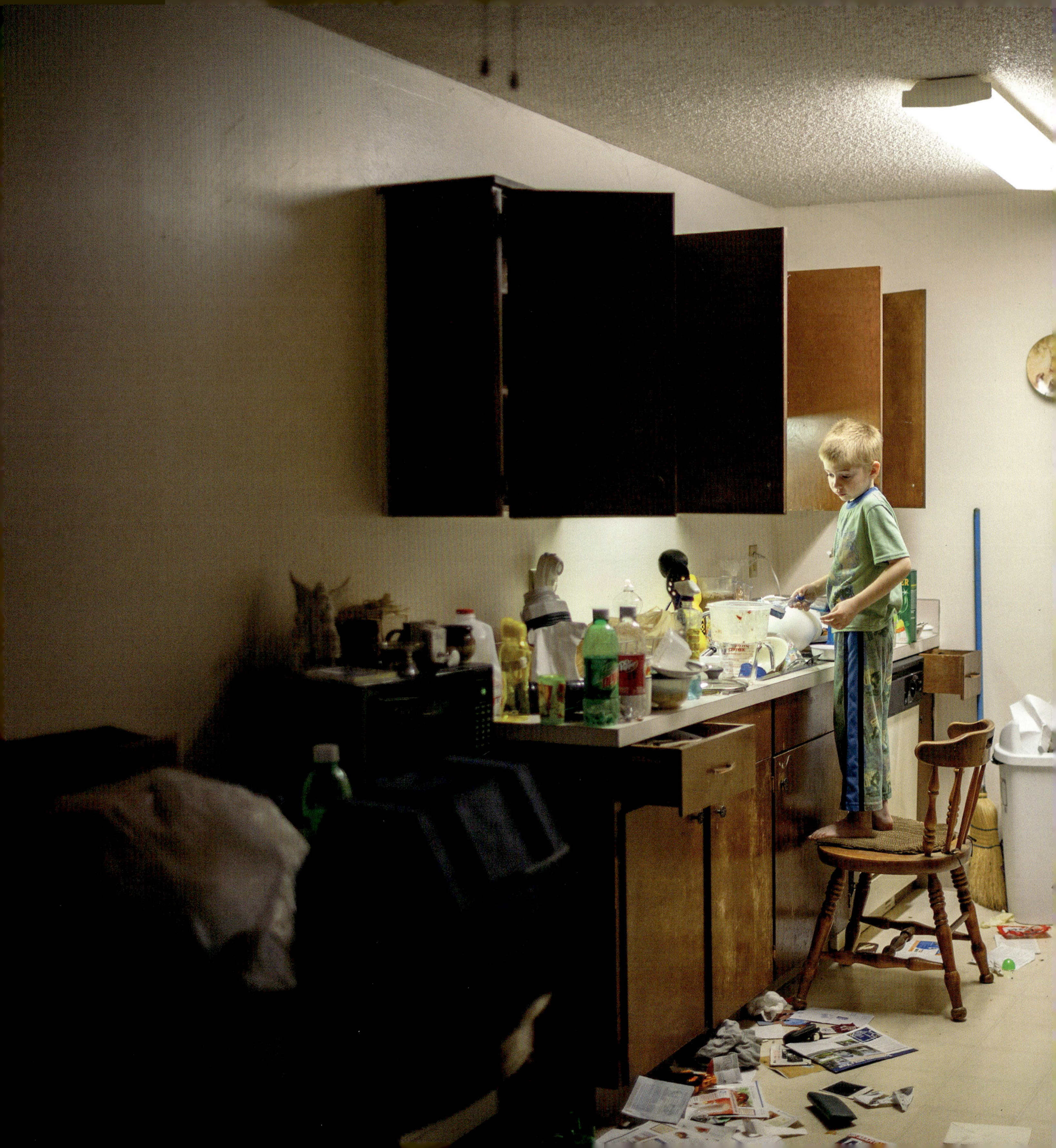

67

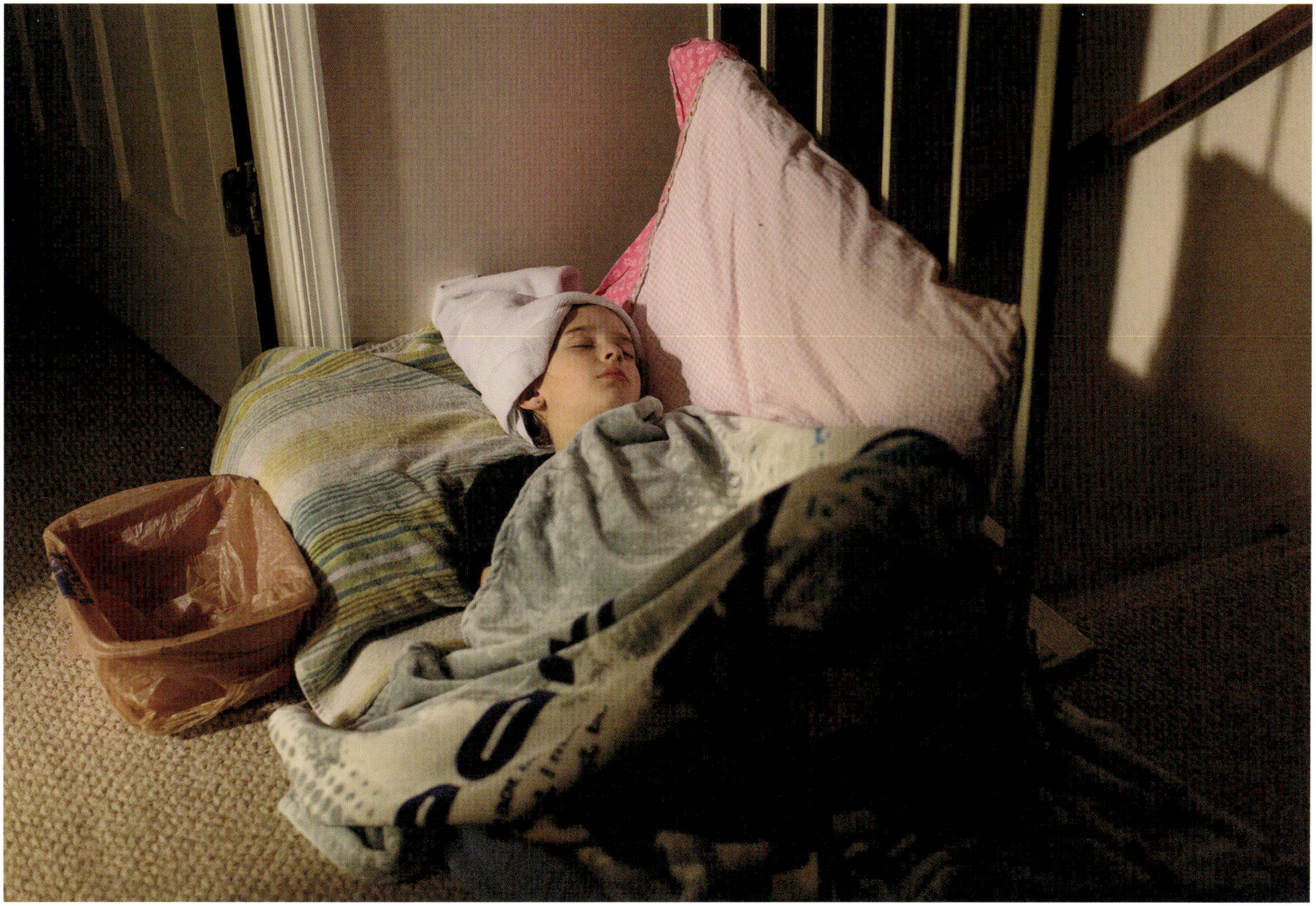

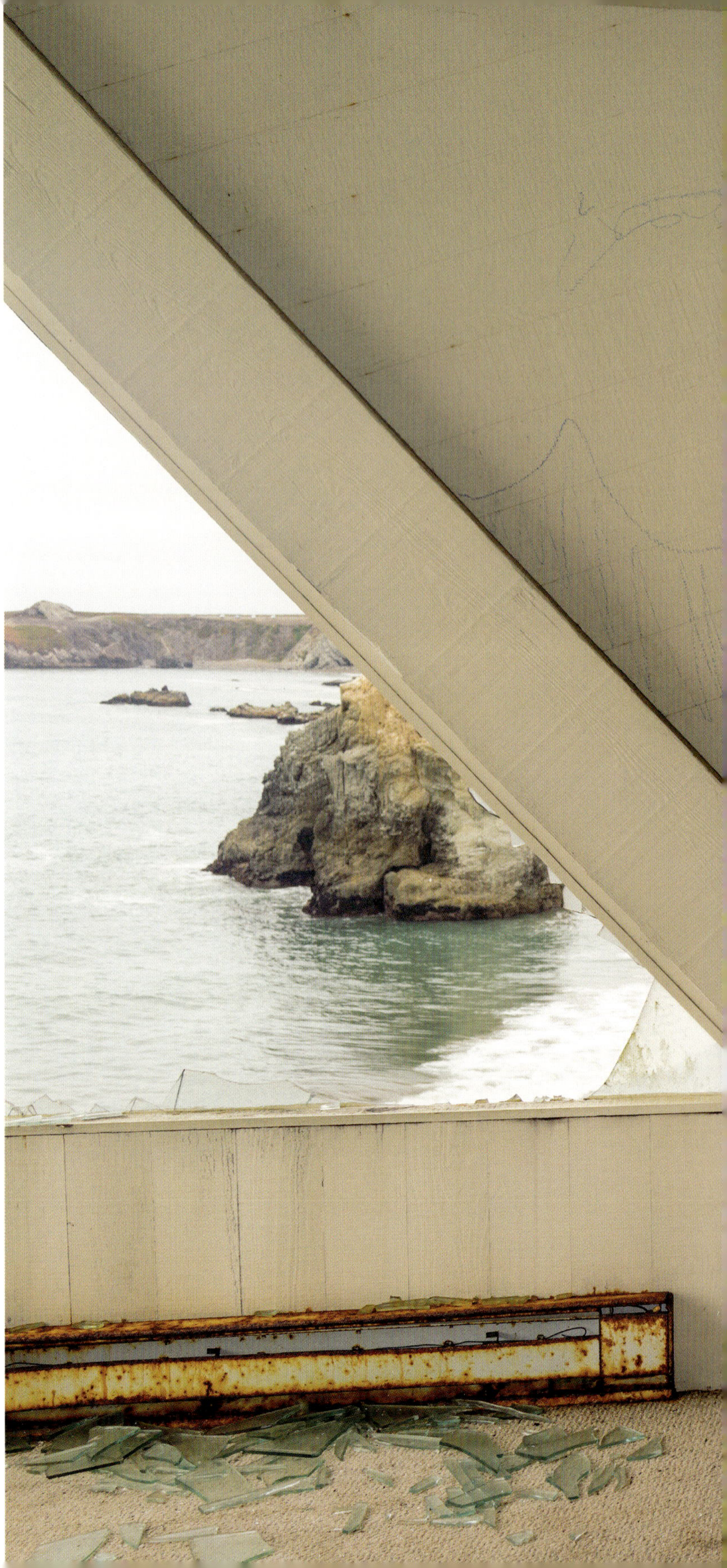

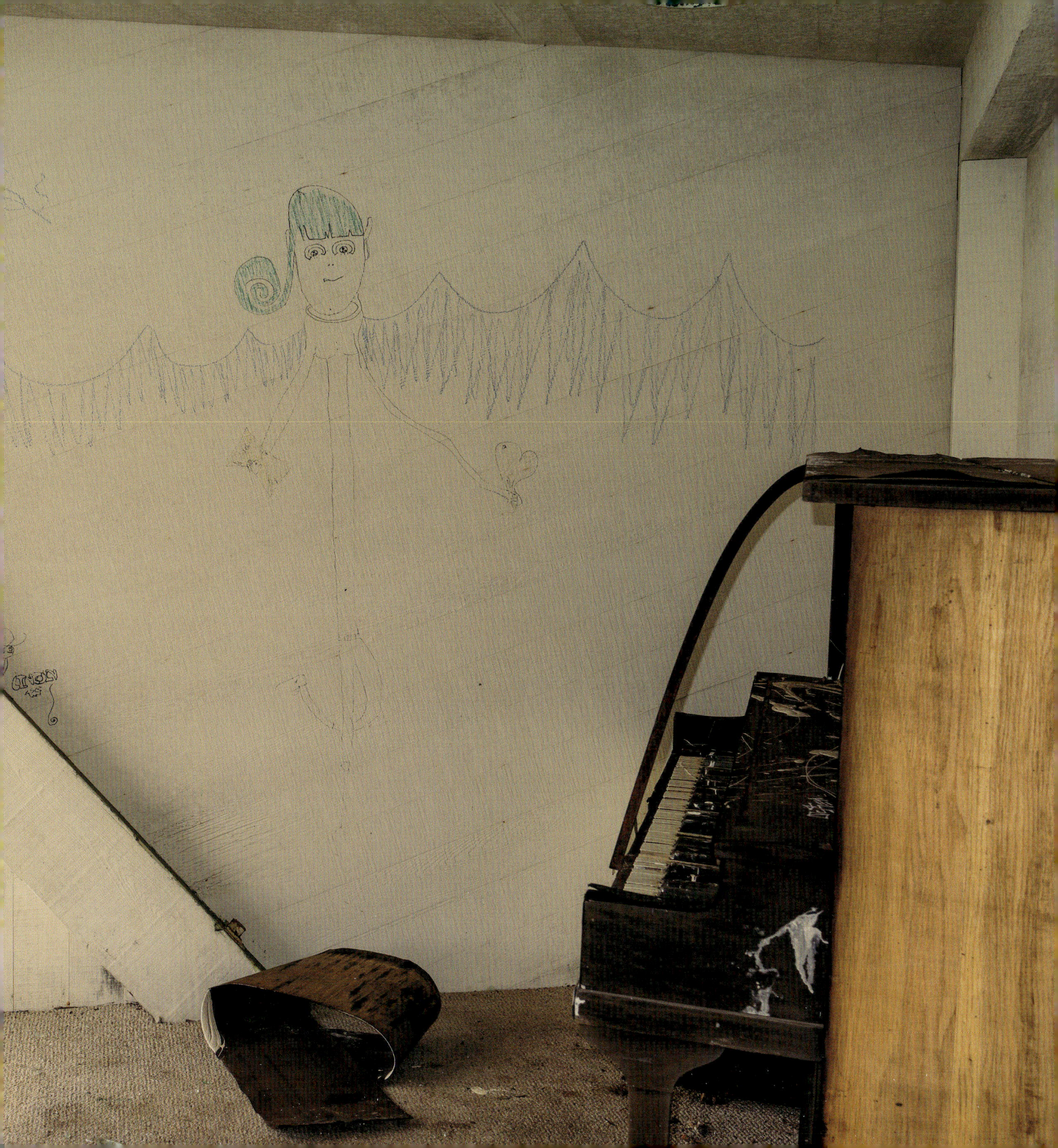

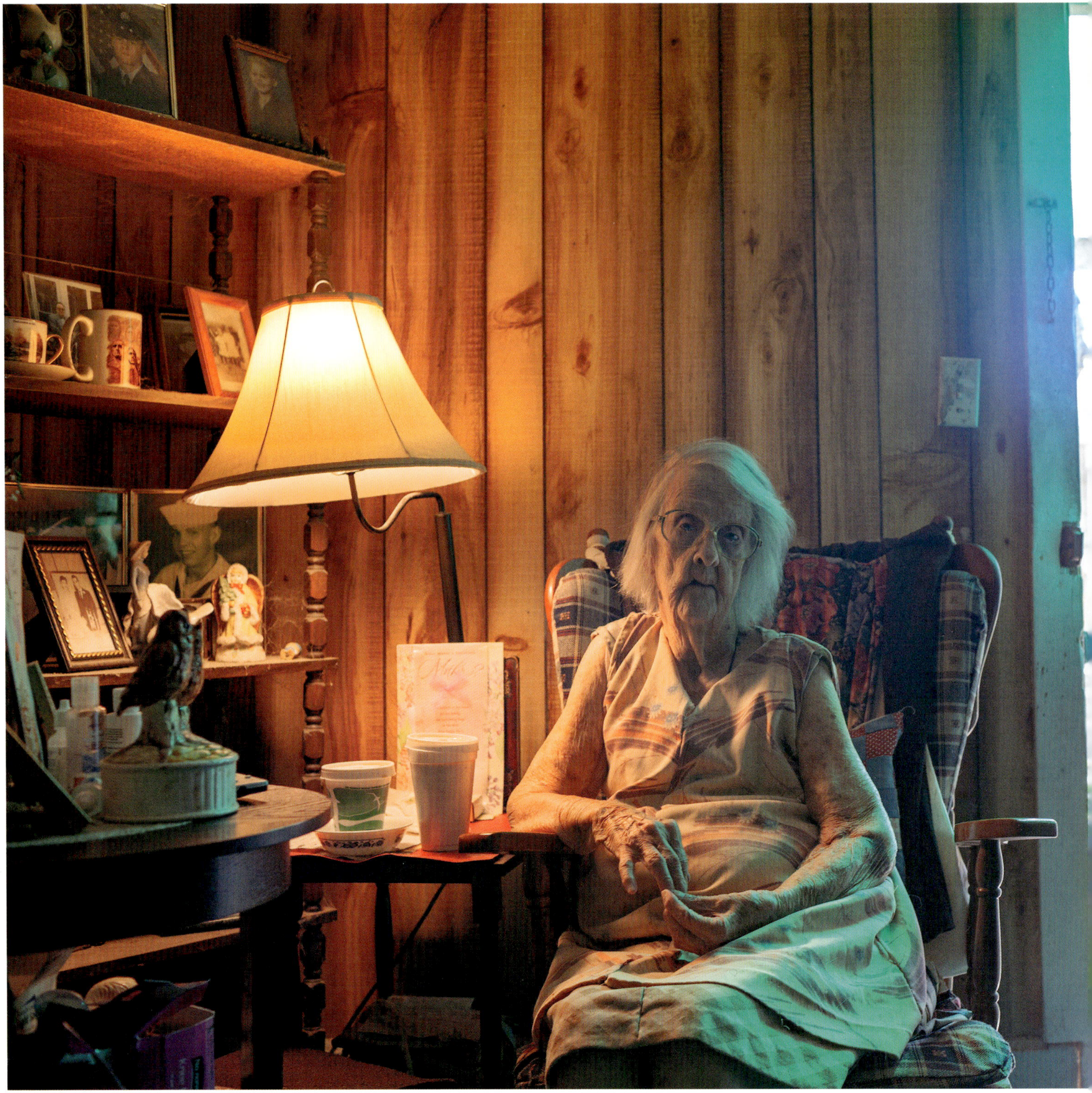

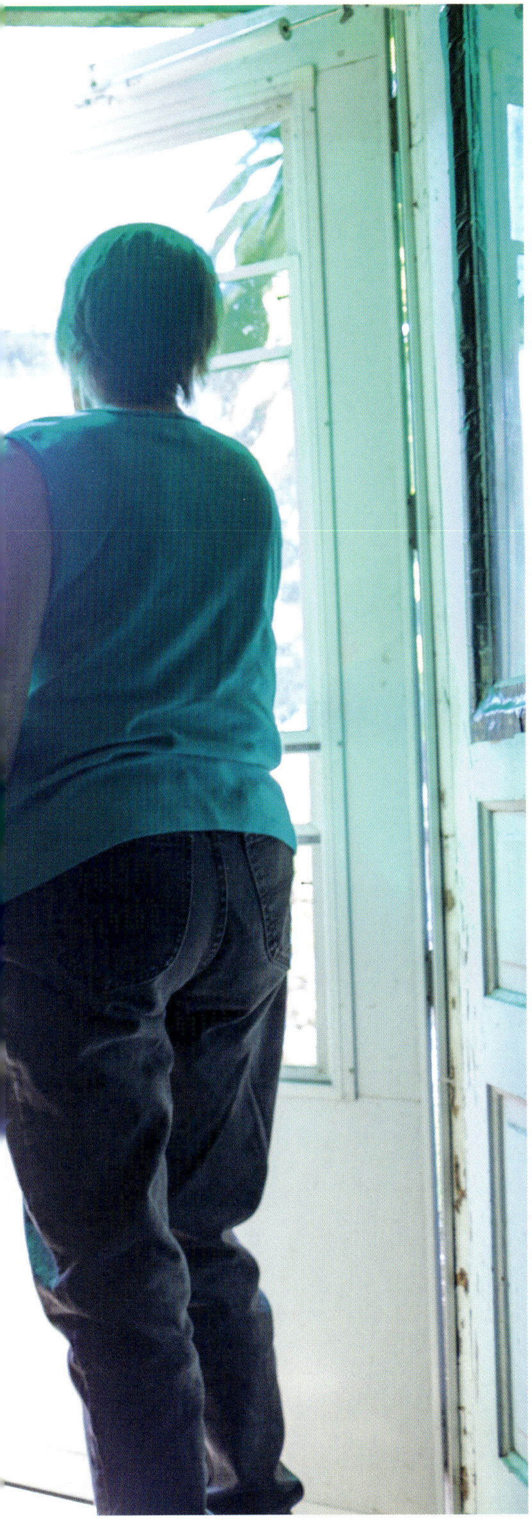

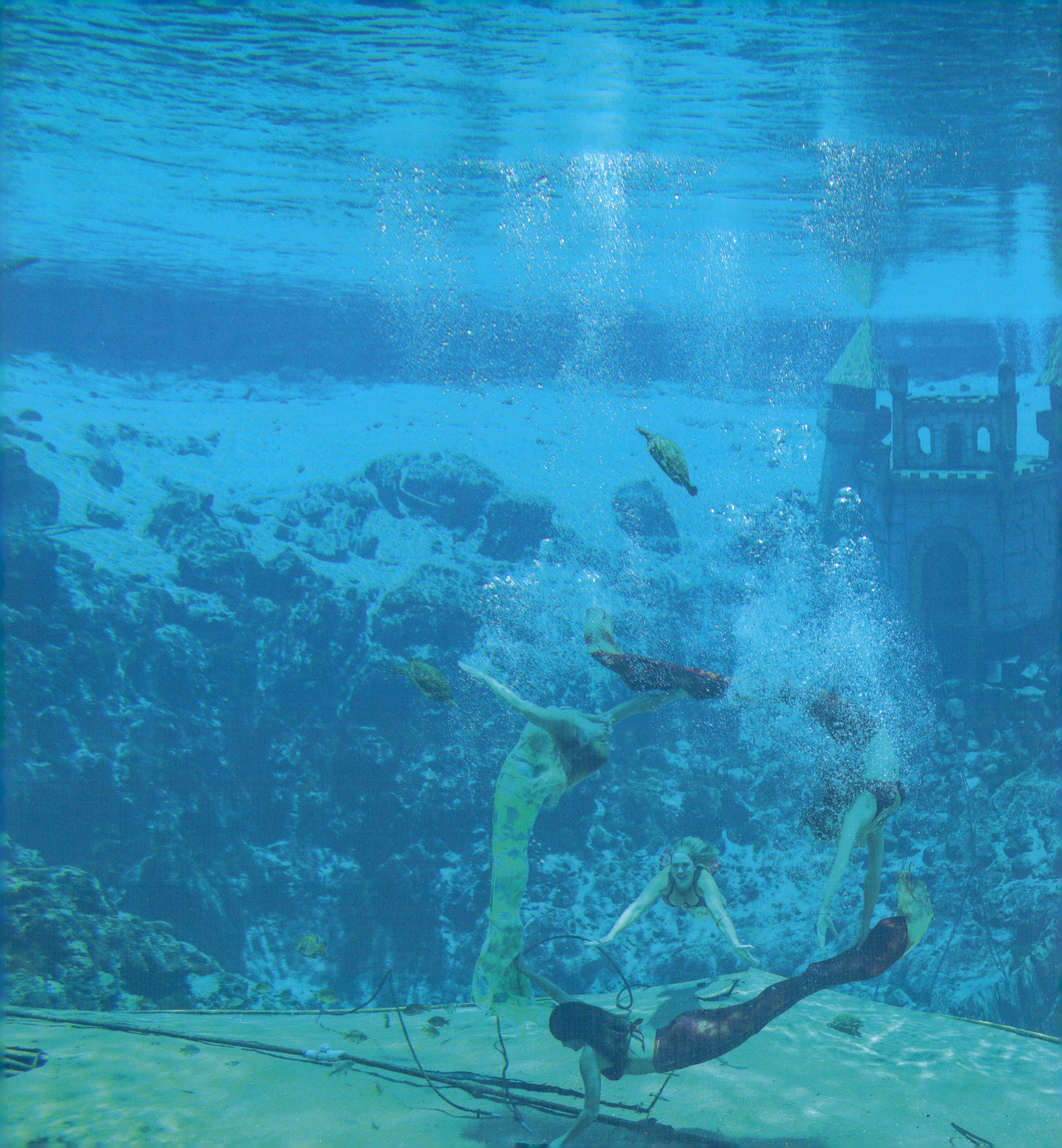

75

77

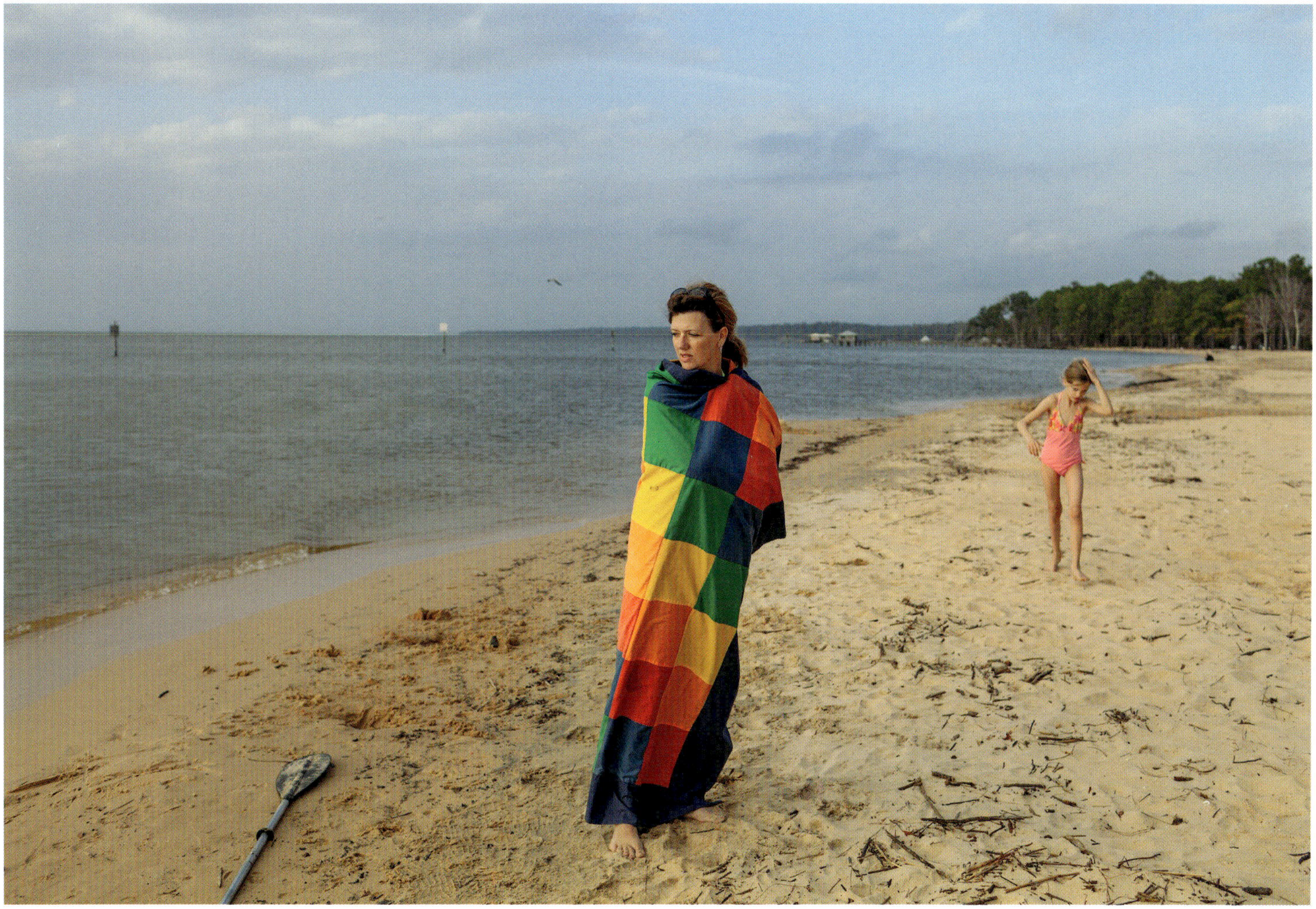

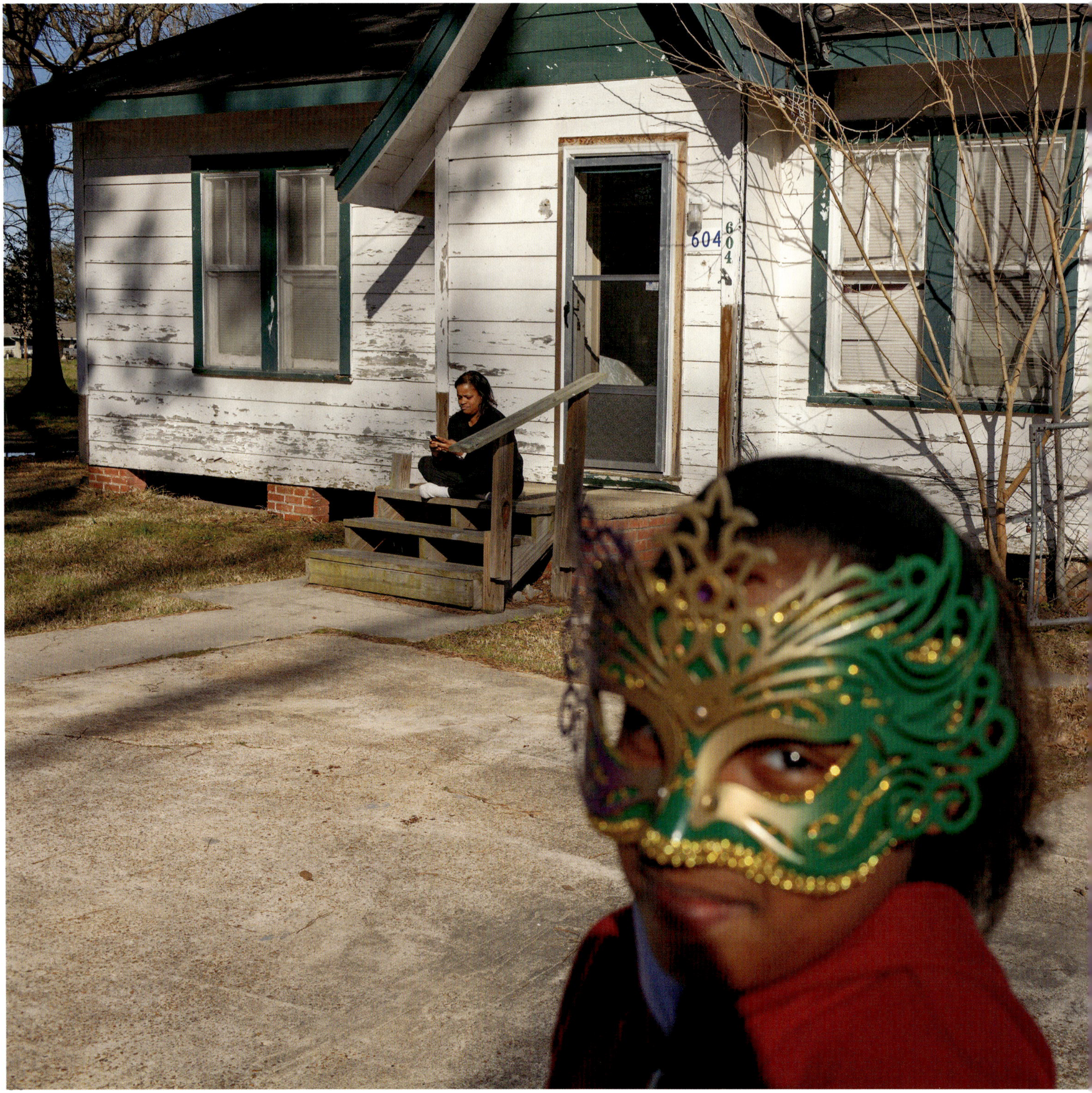
604
604

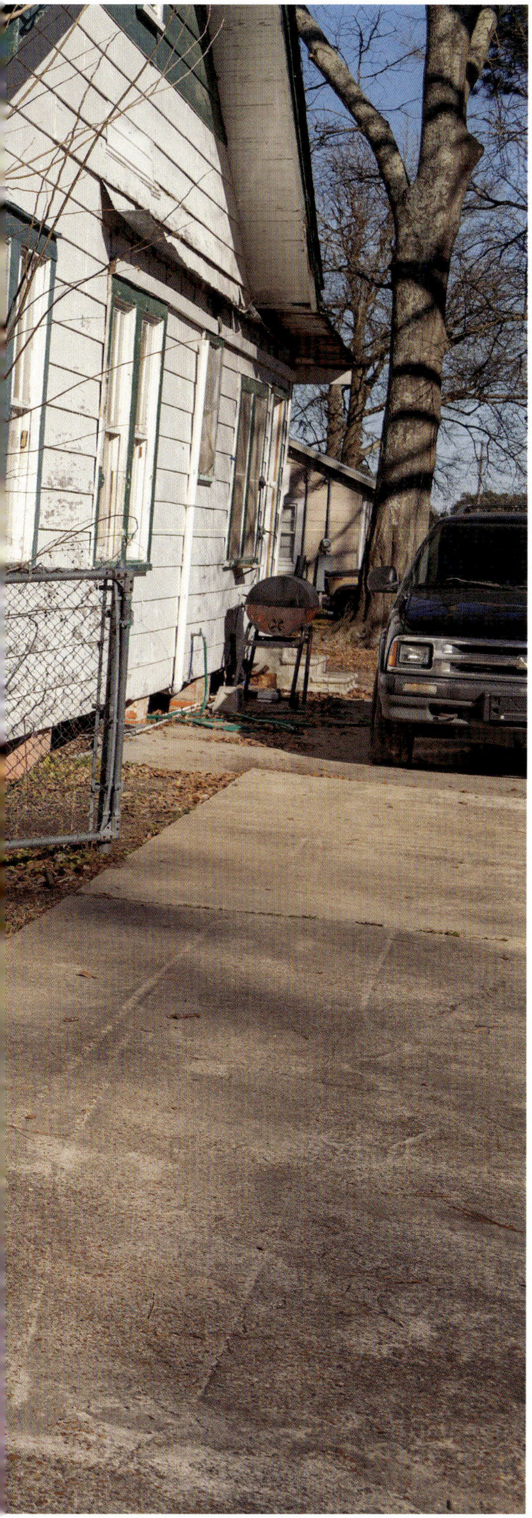

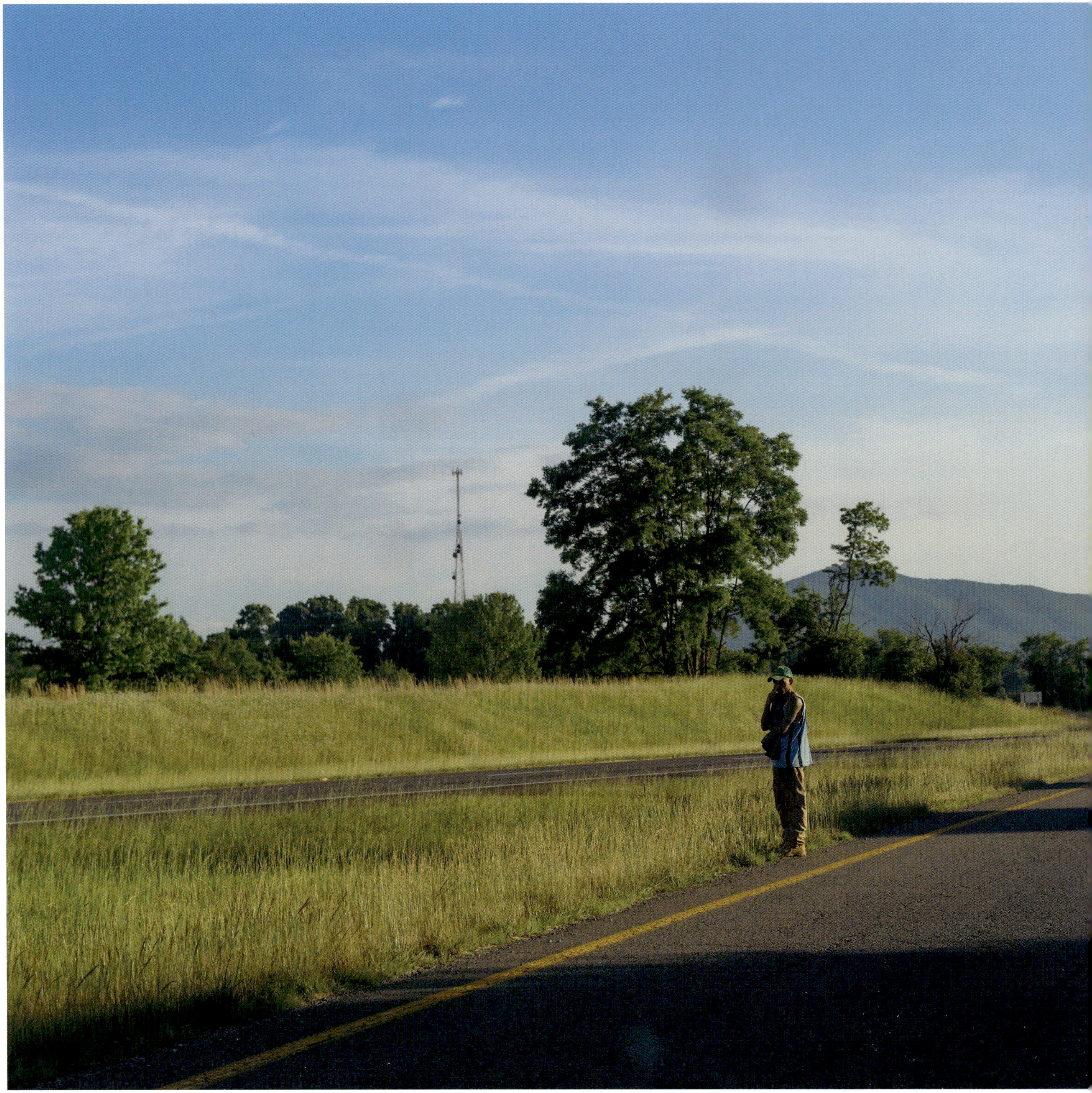

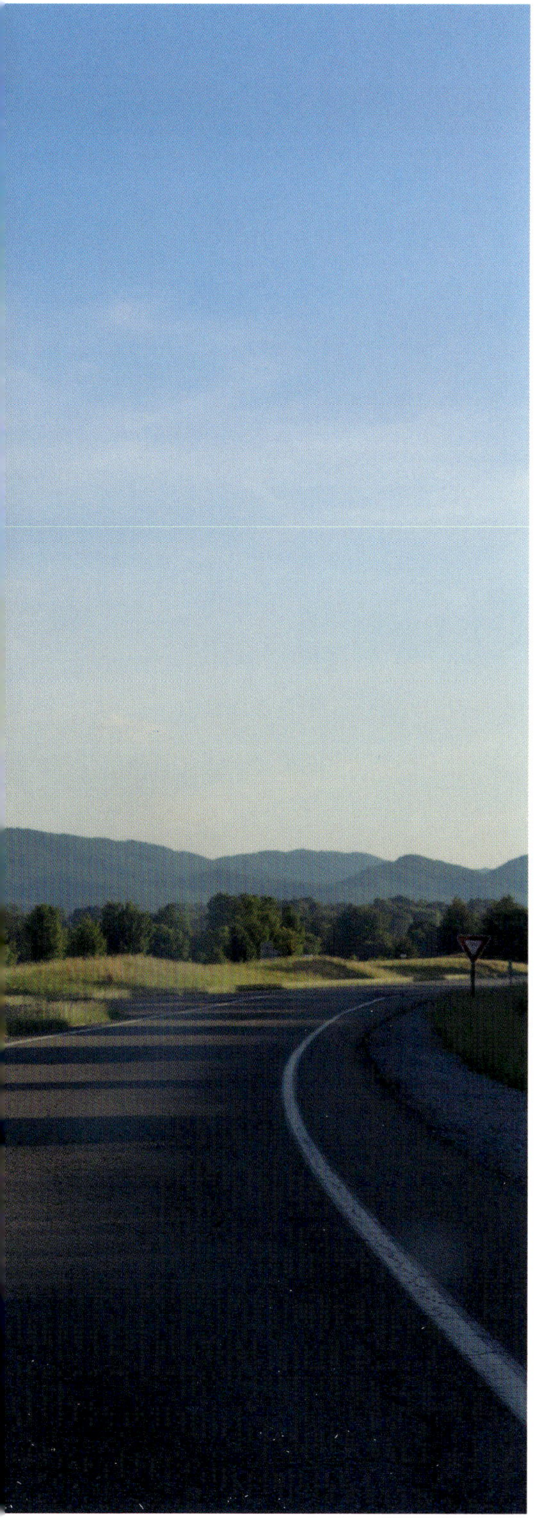

85

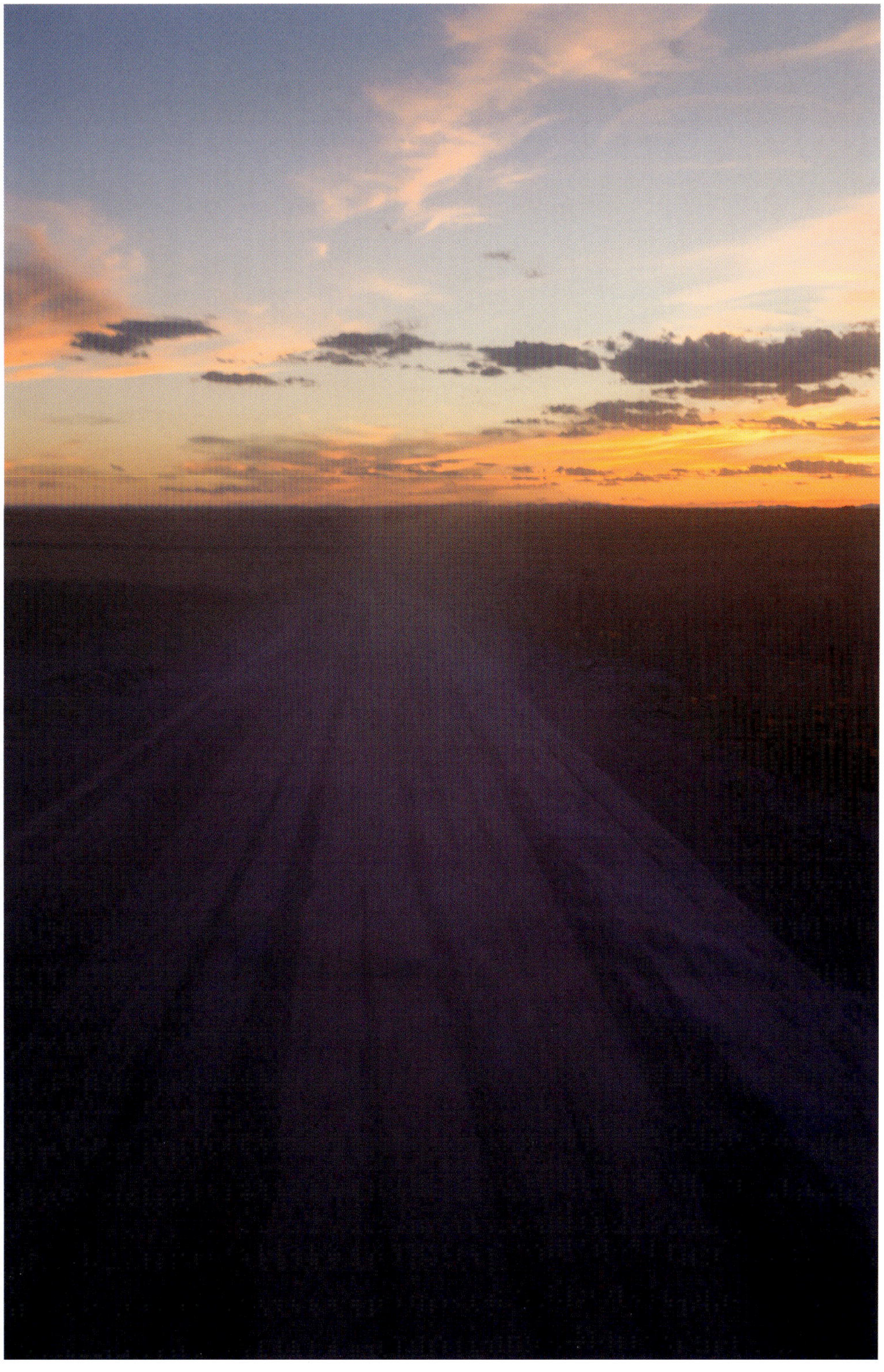

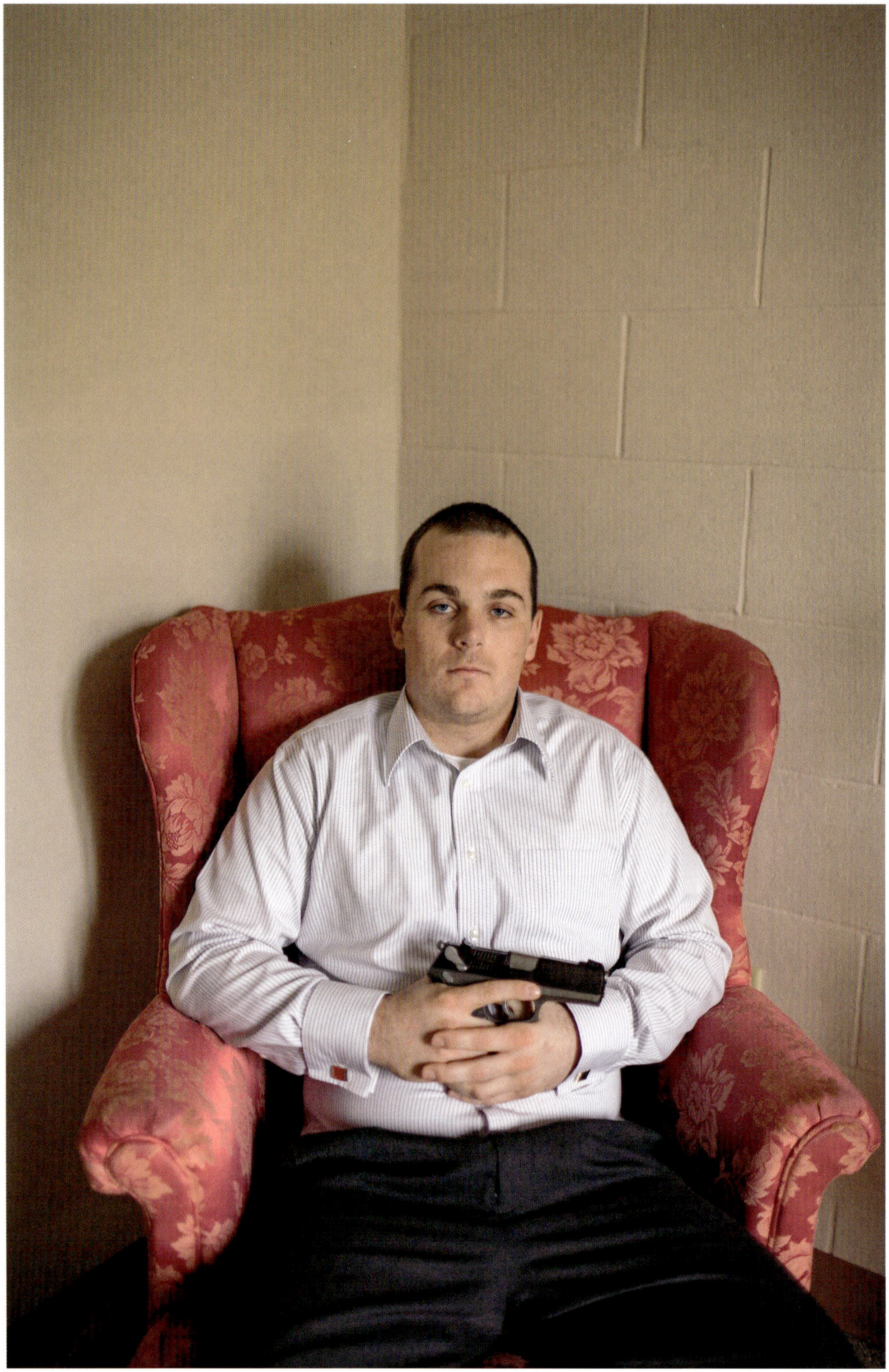

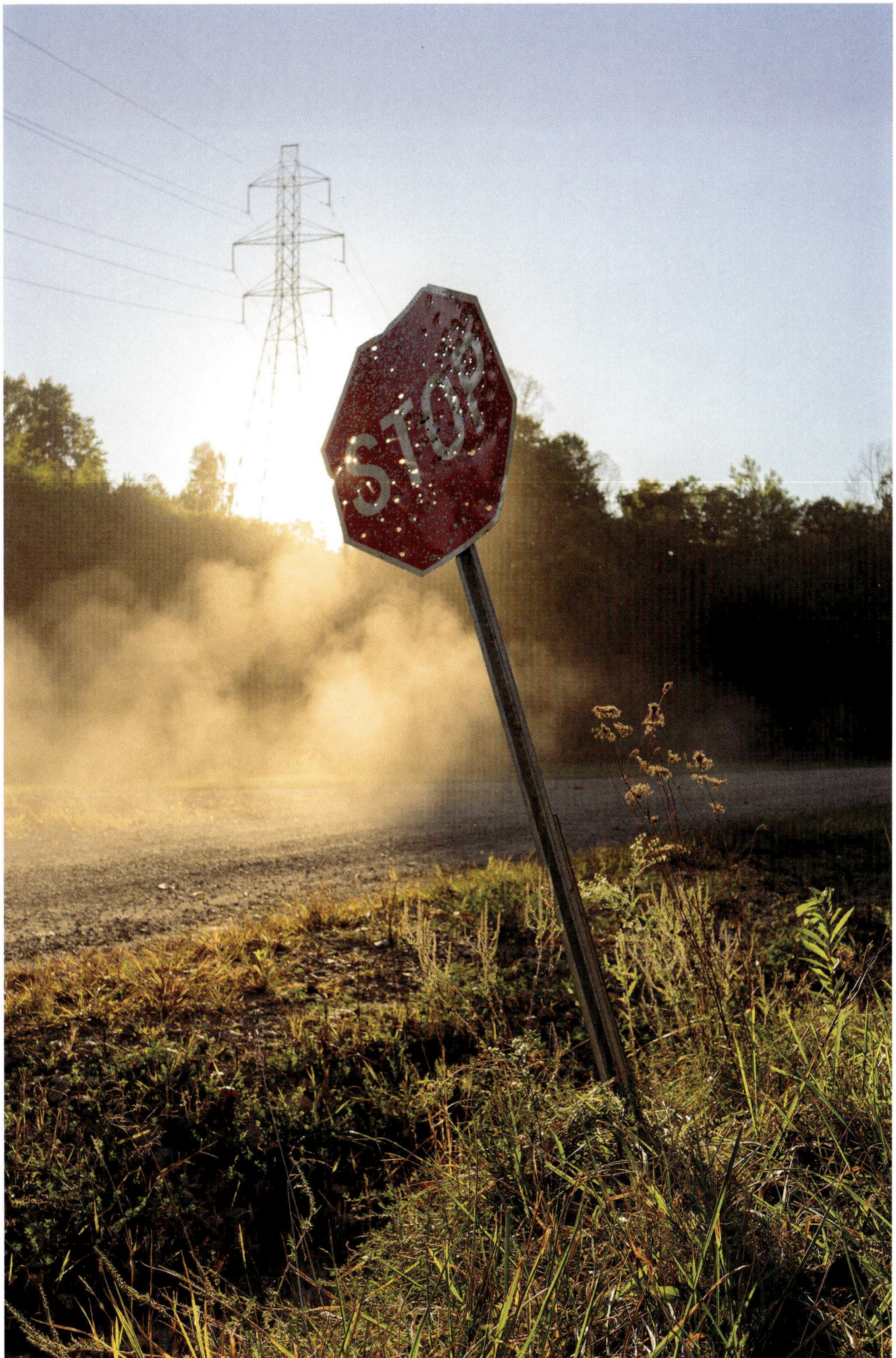
STOP

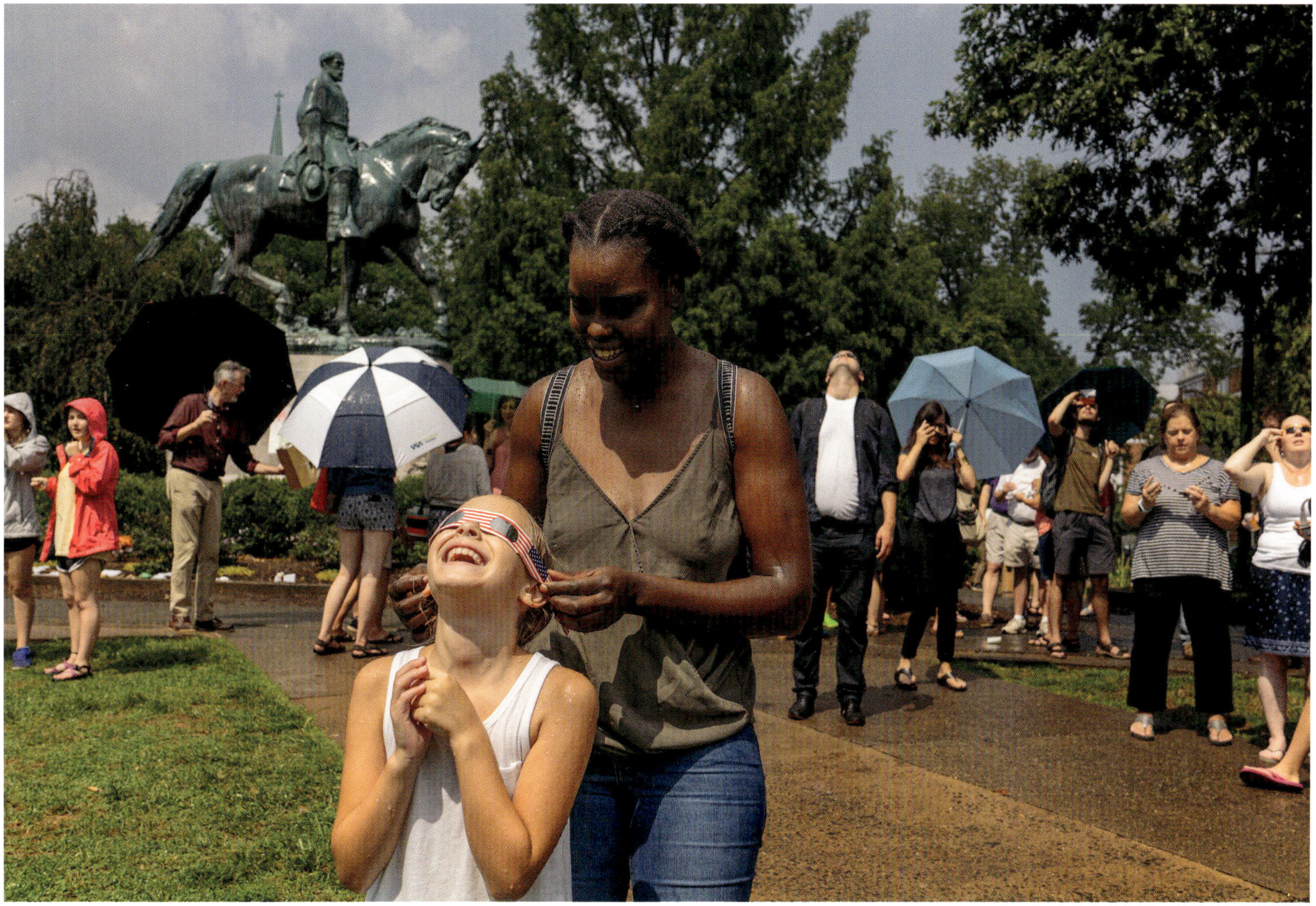

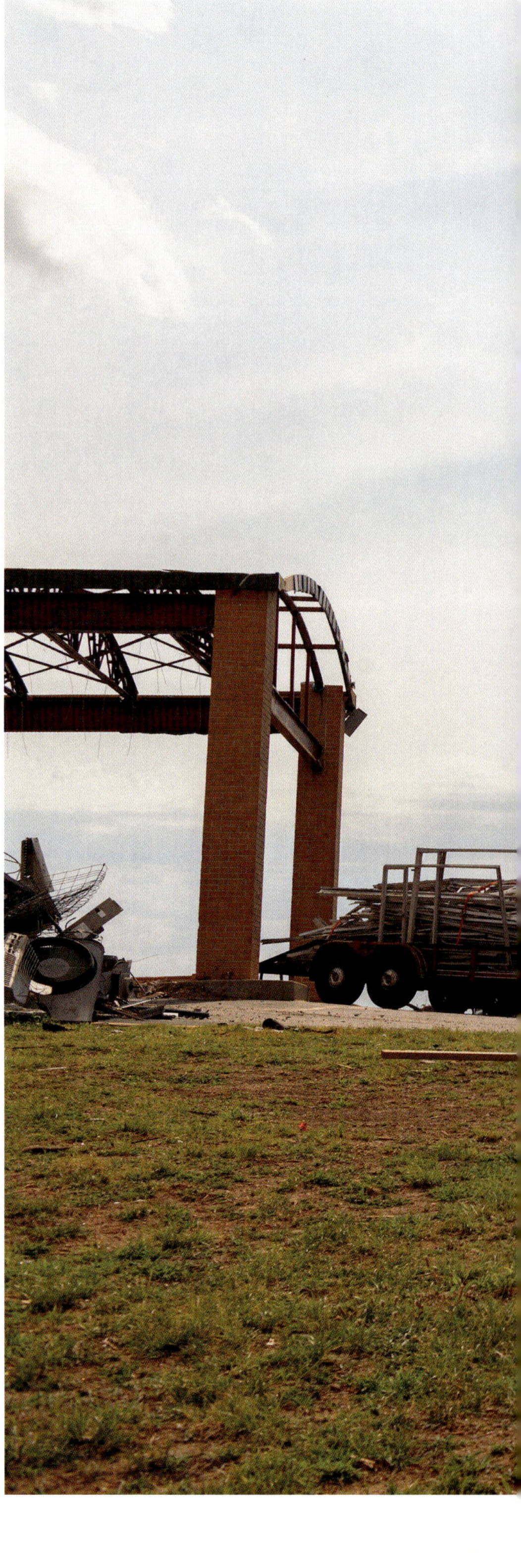

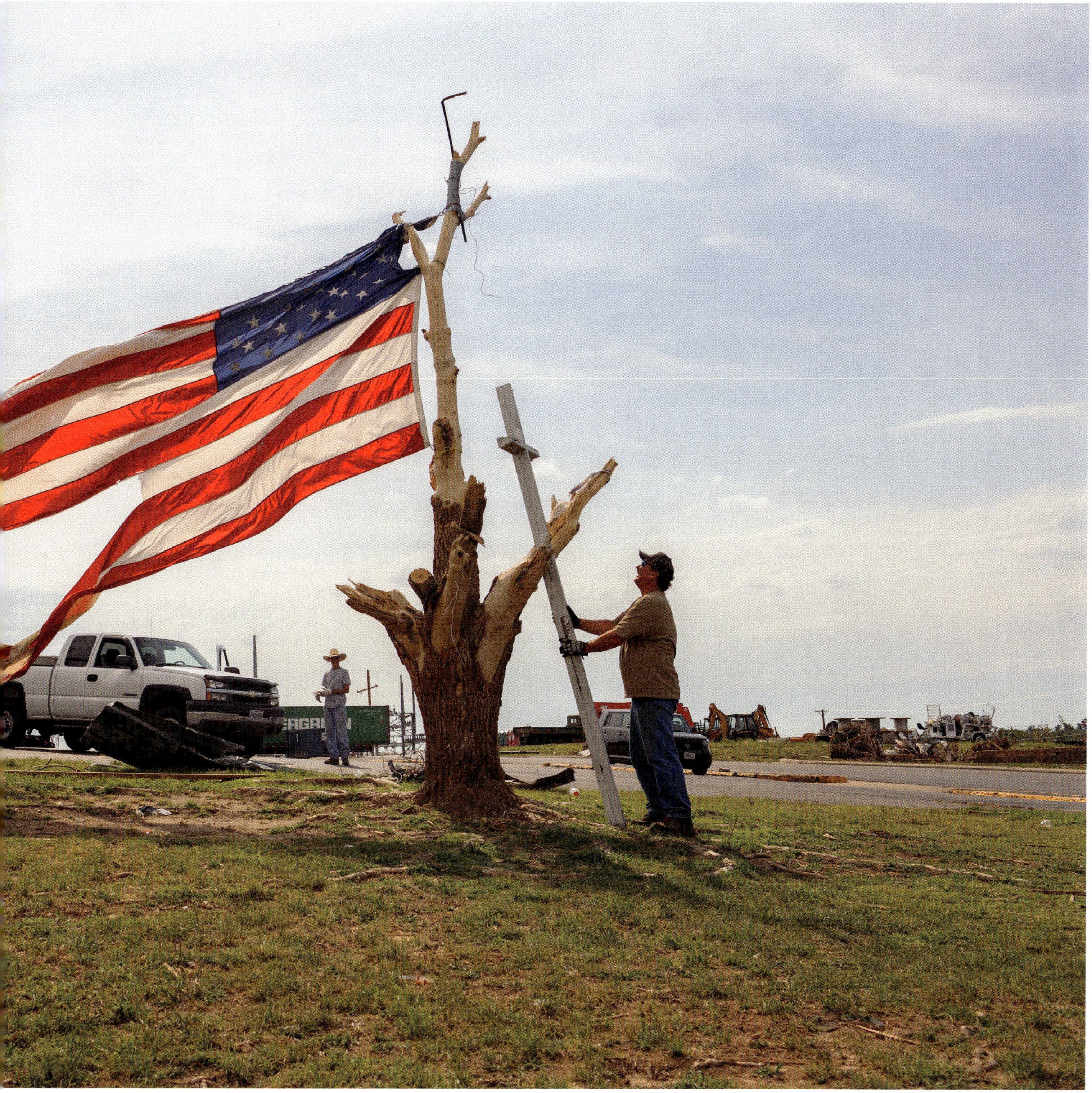

94

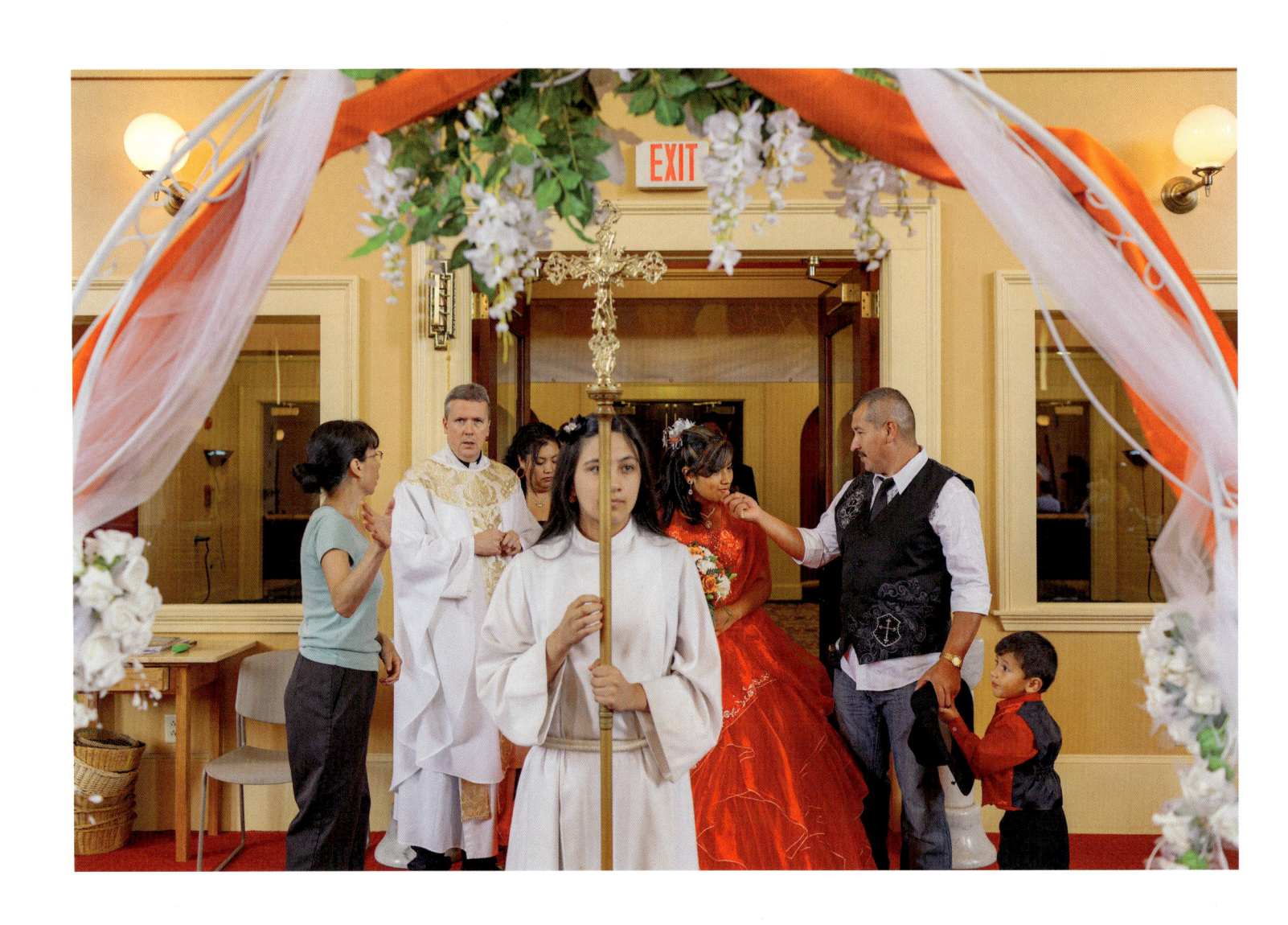

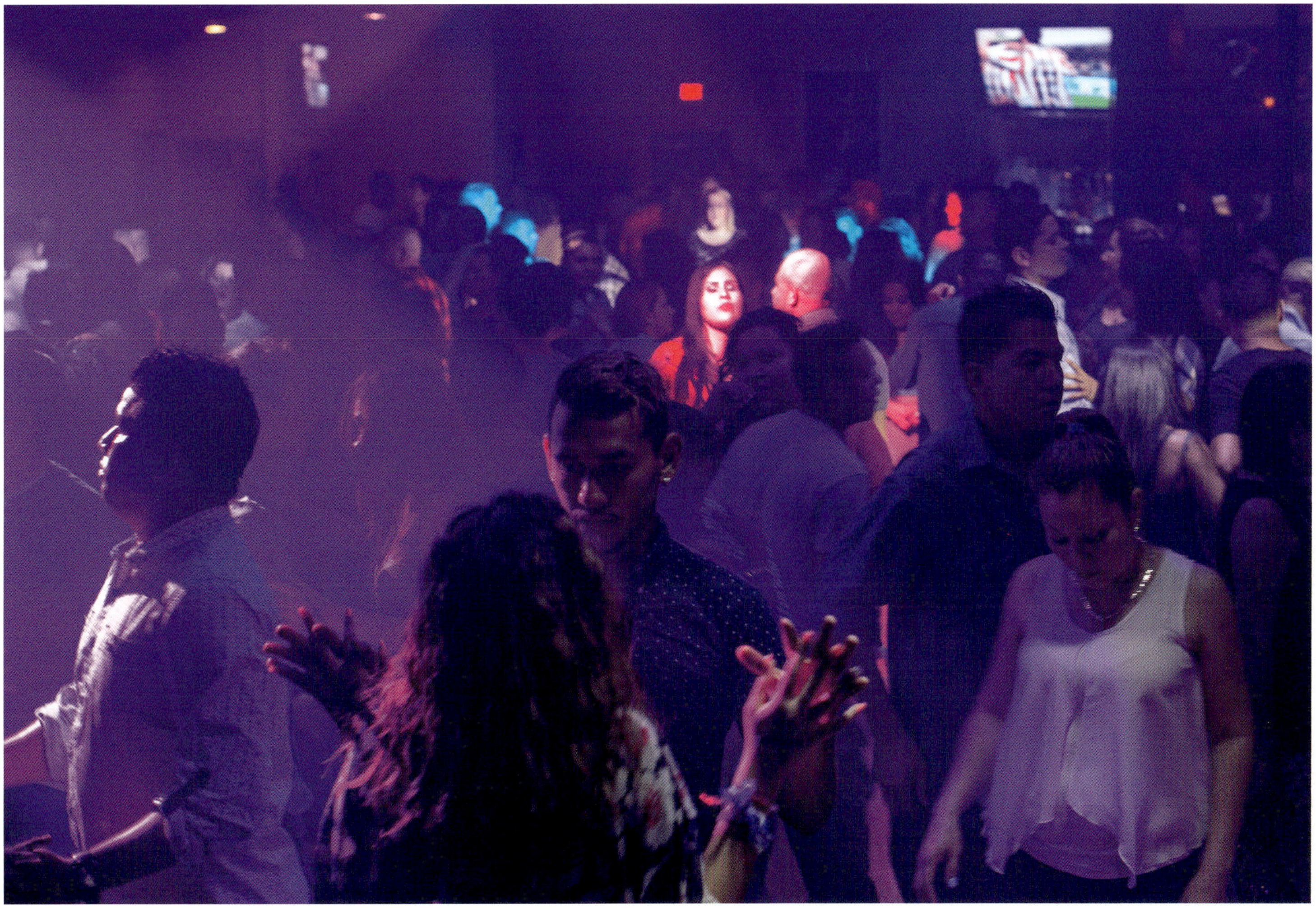

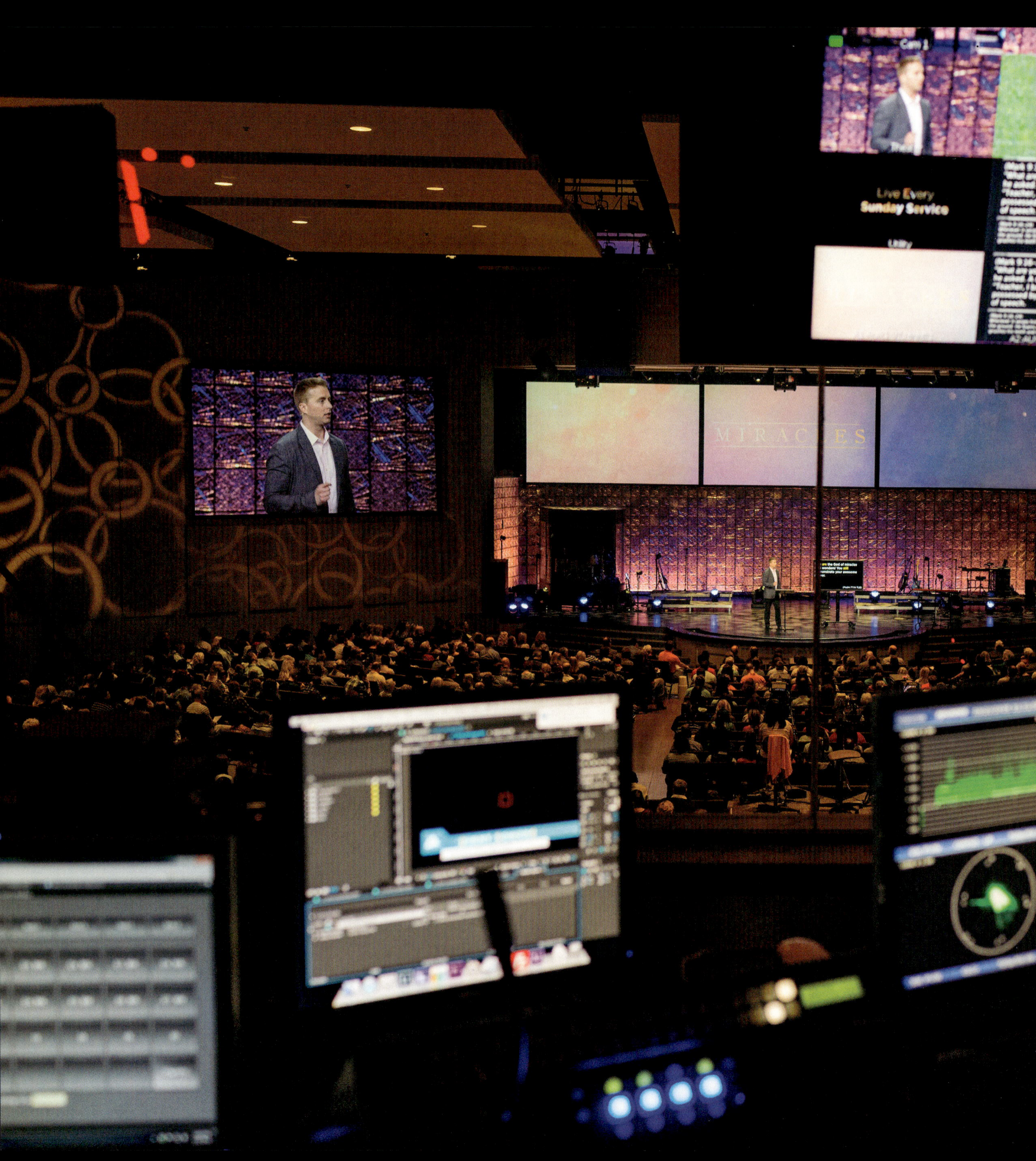
Live Every
Sunday Service
MIRACLES

97

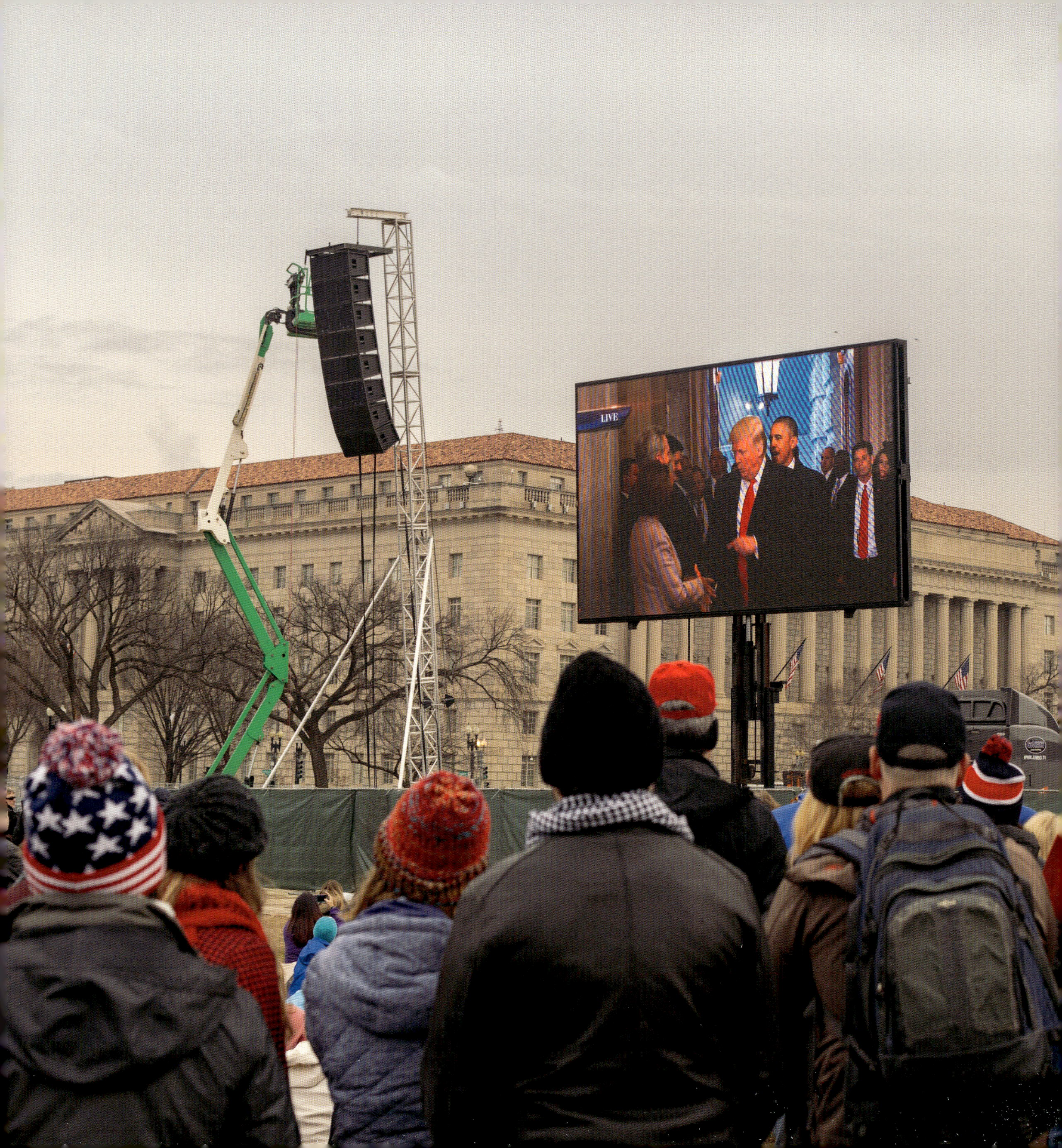
LIVE

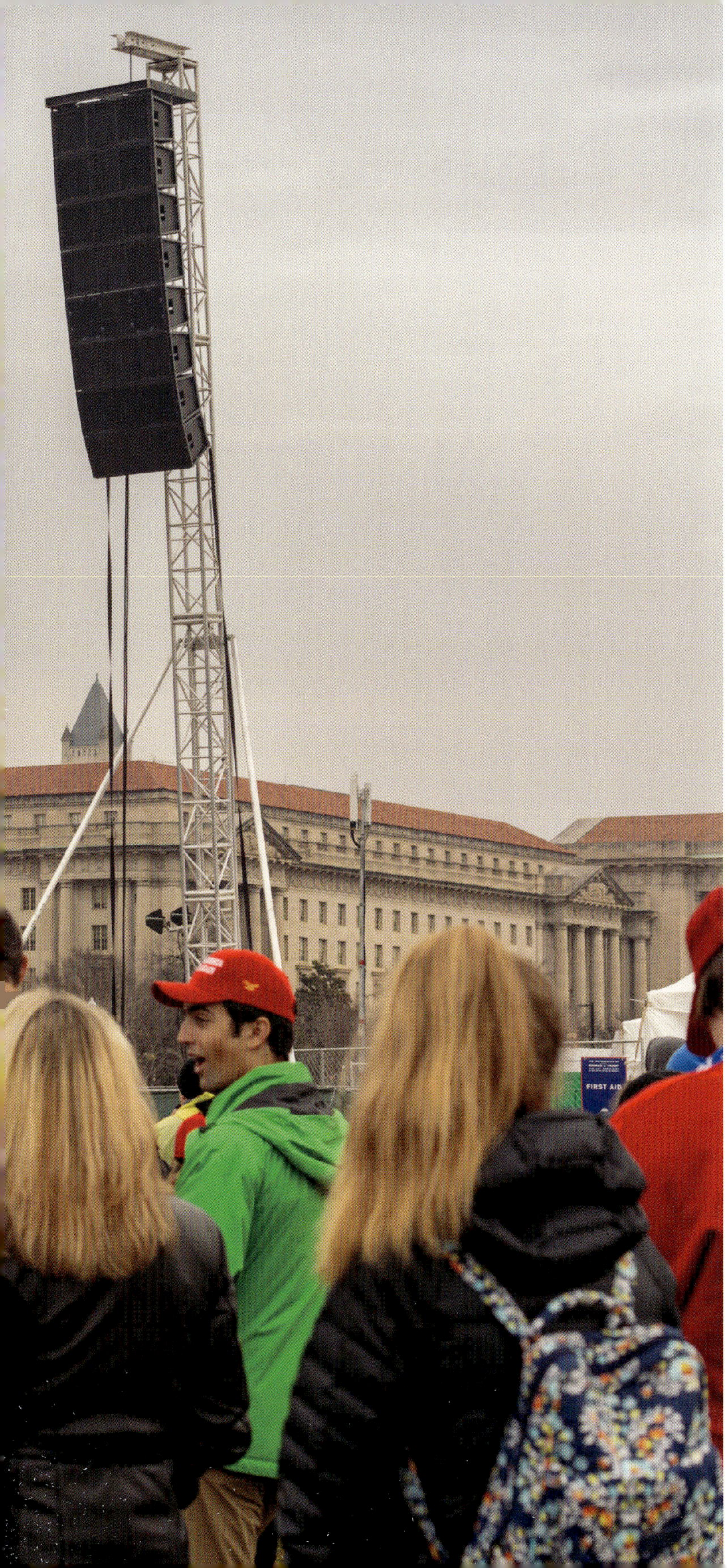
FIRST AID

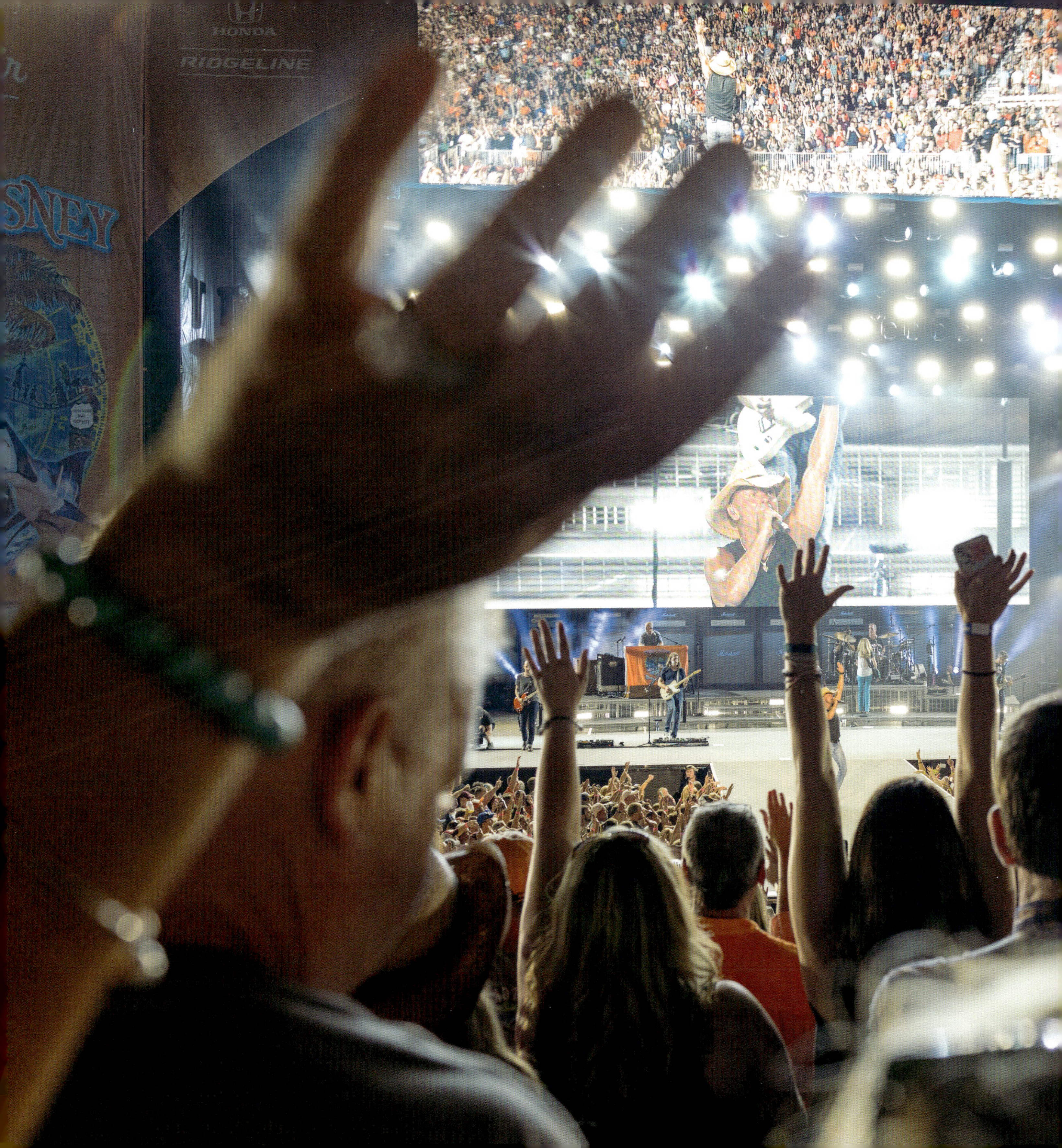
HONDA
RIDGELINE

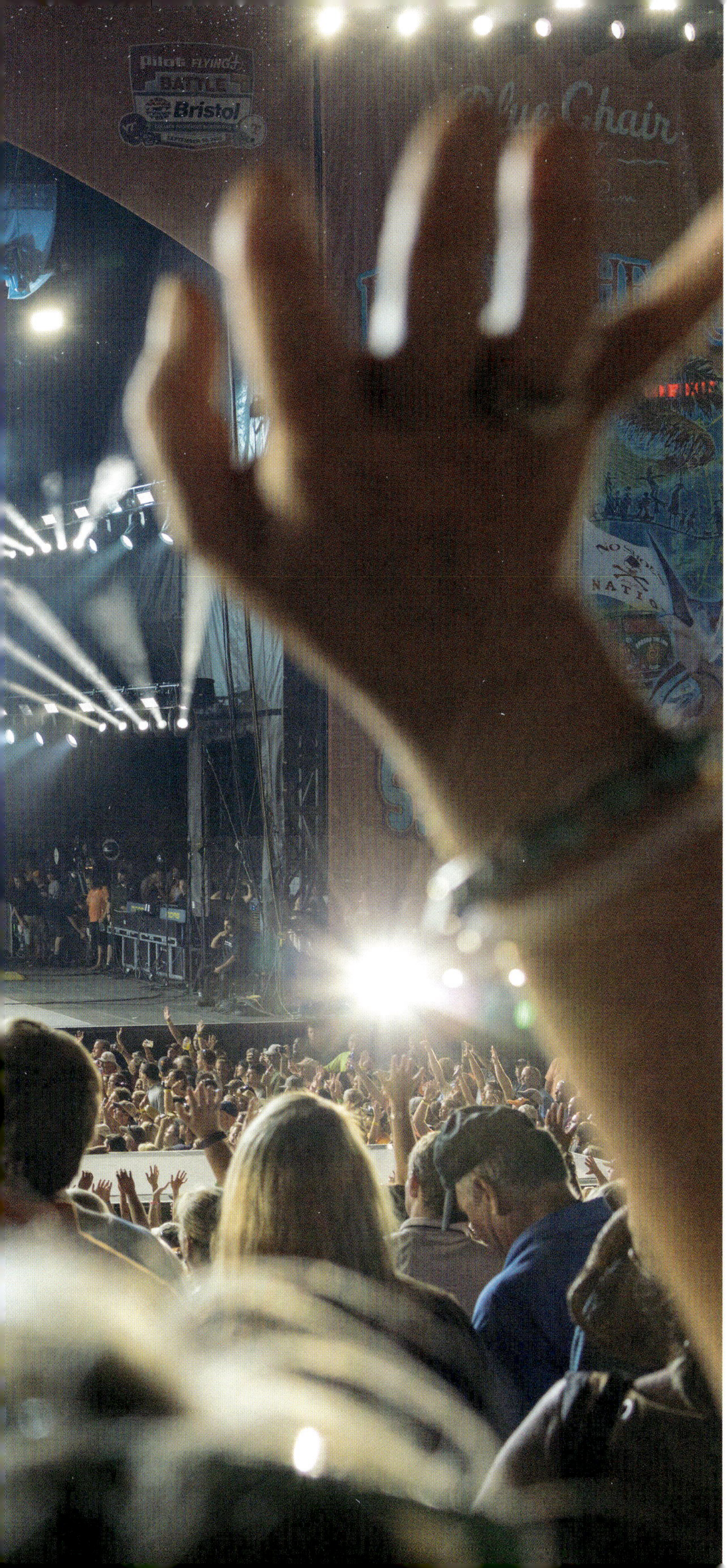
BATTLE
Bristol

103

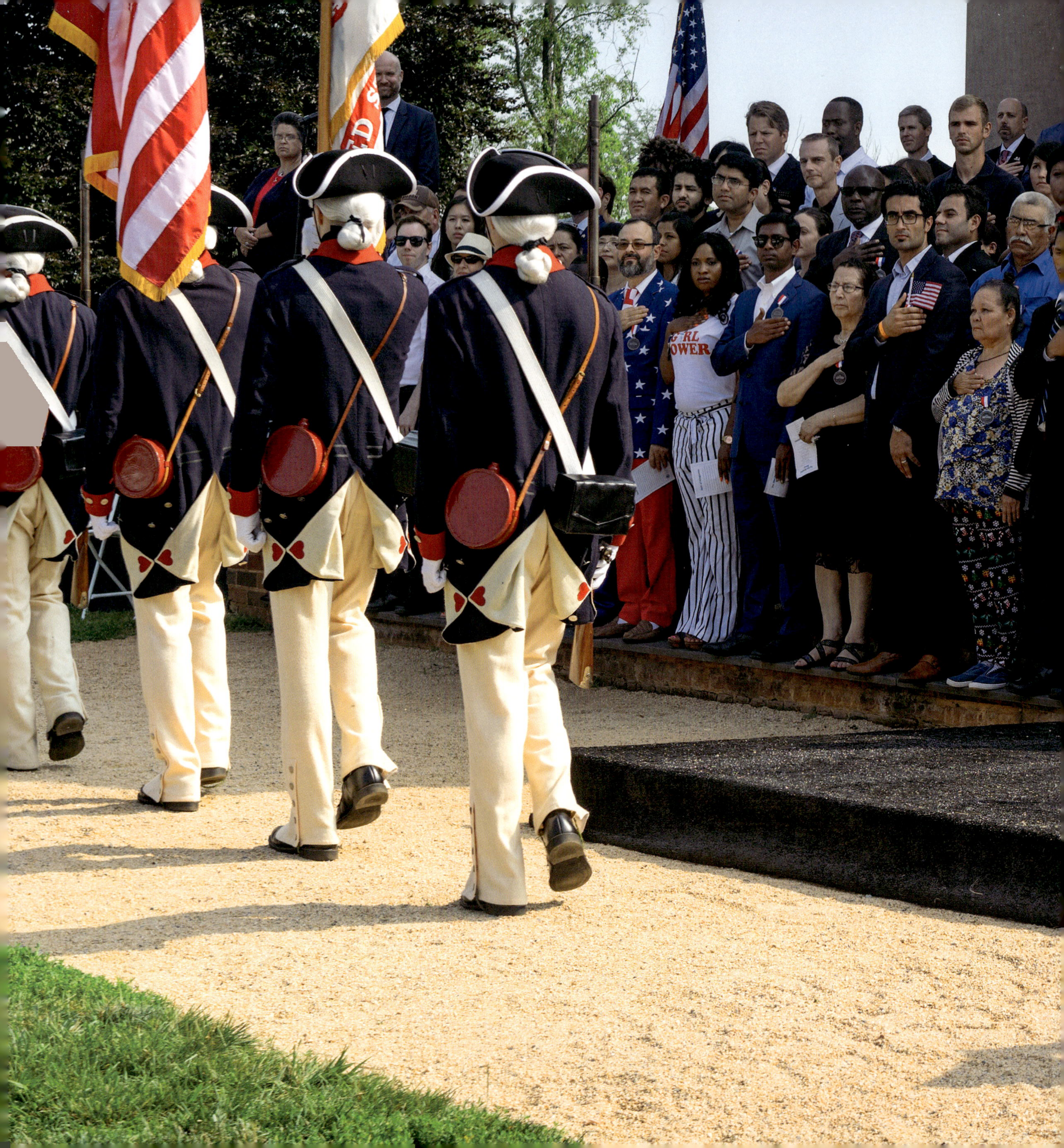

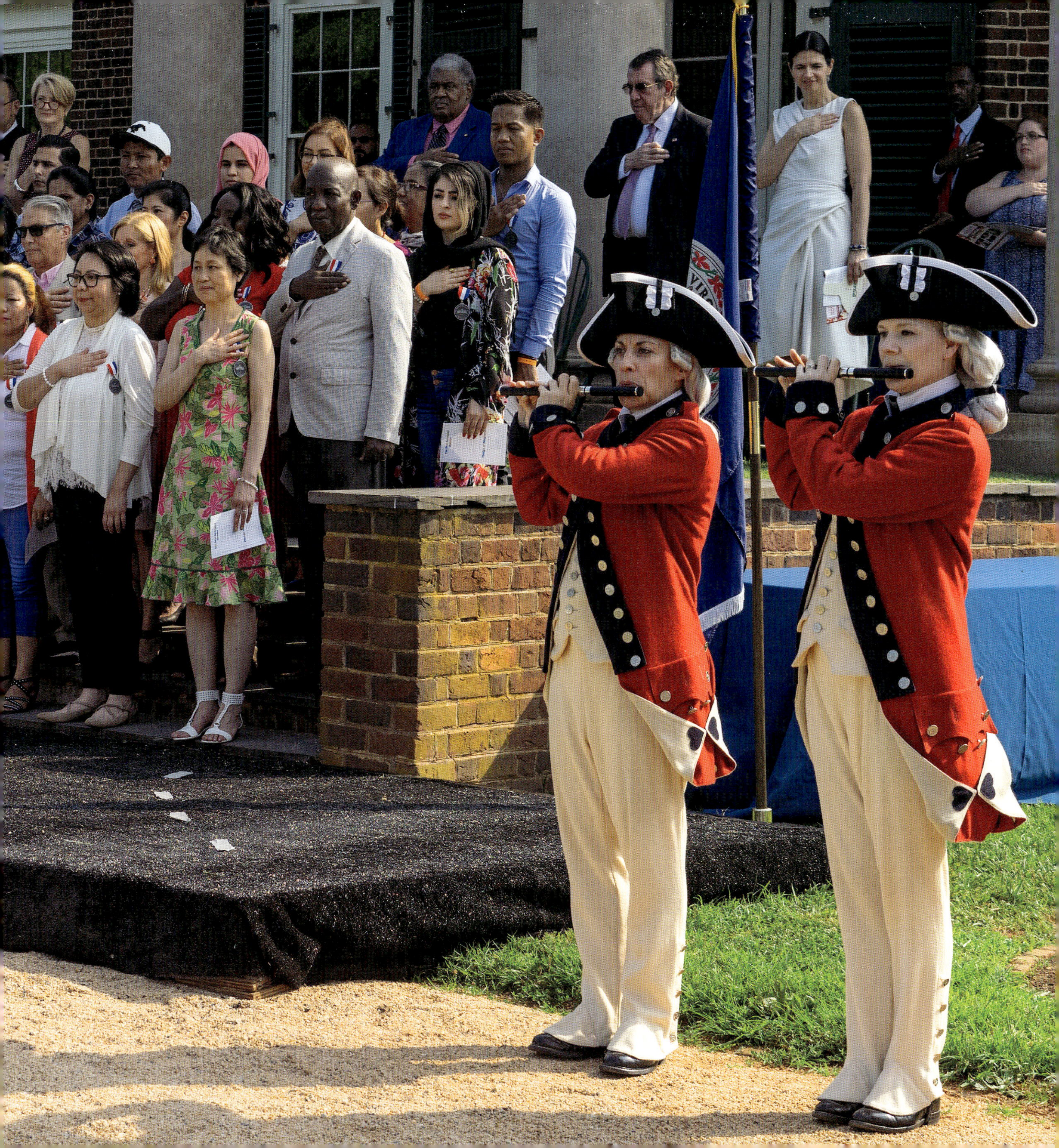

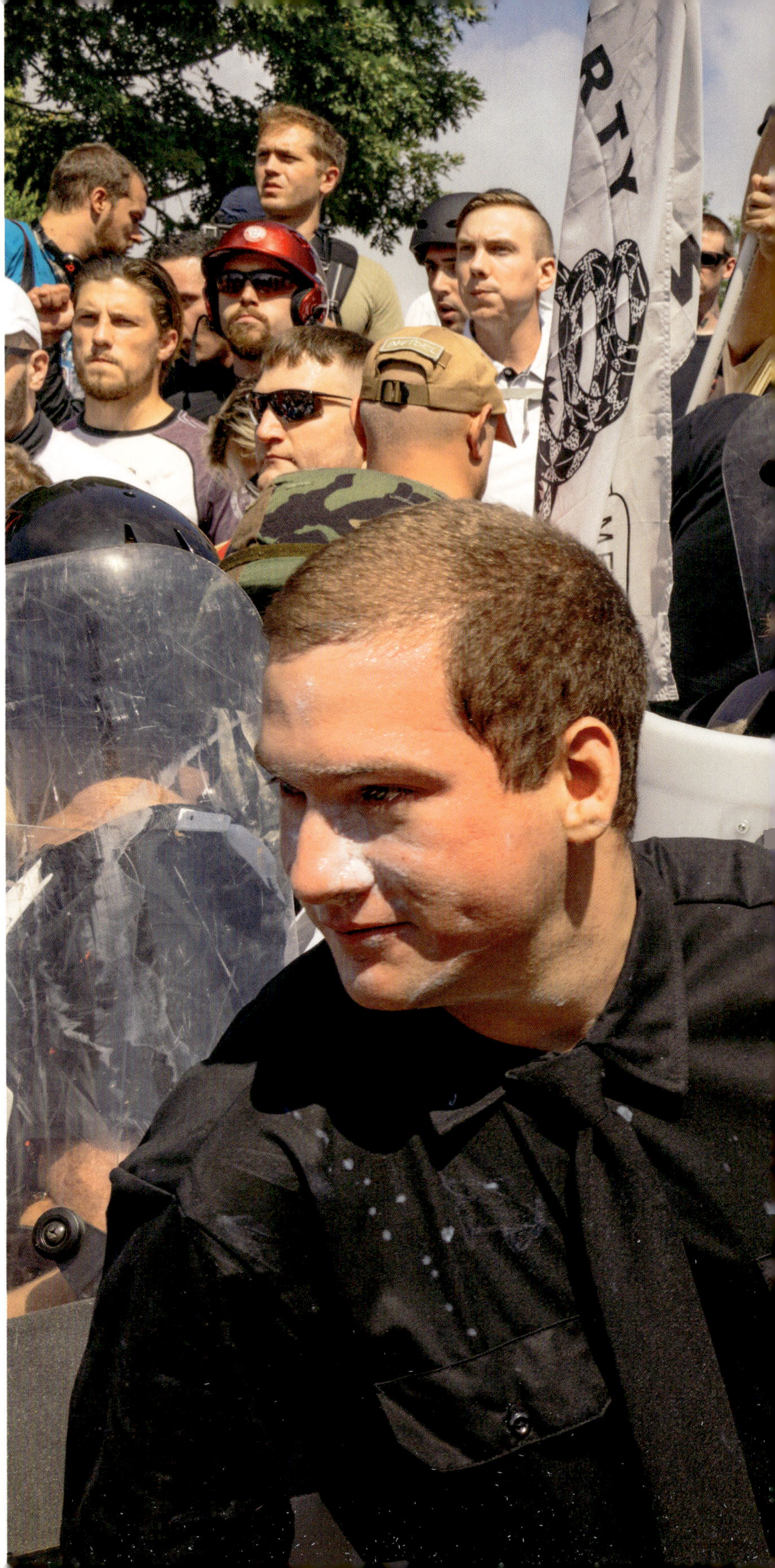

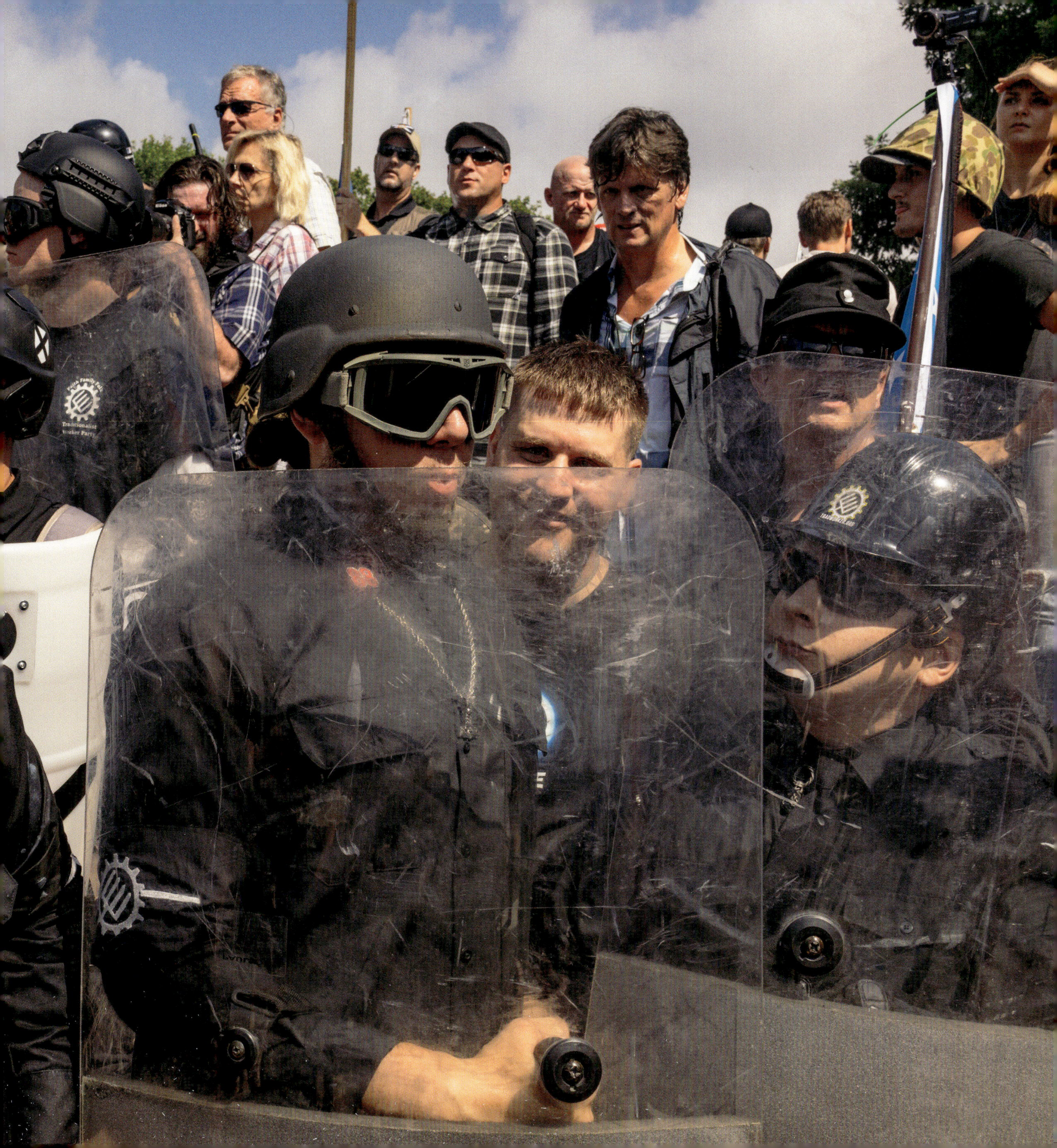

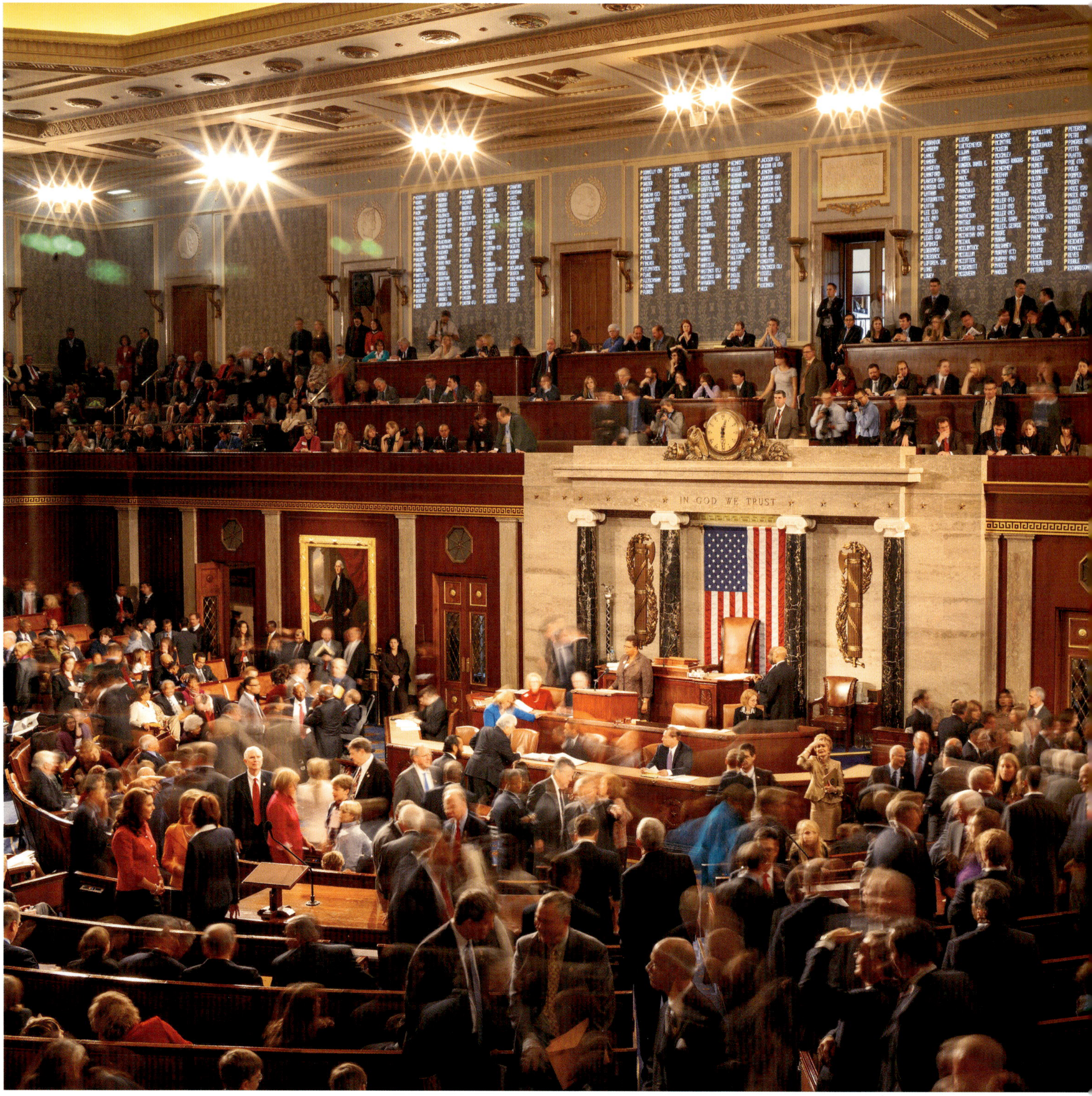
IN GOD WE TRUST

P RICHMOND
P RIGELL
P RIVERA
P ROBY
P ROE (TN)
P ROGERS (AL)
P ROGERS (KY)
P ROGERS (MI)
P ROHRABACHER
P ROKITA
P ROONEY
P ROS-LEHTINEN
P ROSKAM
P ROSS (AR)
P ROSS (FL)
P ROTHMAN (NJ)
P ROYBAL-ALLARD
P ROYCE
P RUNYAN
P RUPPERSBERGER
P RUSH
P RYAN (OH)
P RYAN (WI)
SANCHEZ, LINDA T.
P SANCHEZ, LORETTA
P SARBANES
P SCALISE
P SCHAKOWSKY
P SCHIFF
P SCHILLING
P SCHMIDT
P SCHOCK
P SCHRADER
P SCHWARTZ
P SCHWEIKERT
P SCOTT (SC)
P SCOTT (VA)
P SCOTT, AUSTIN
P SCOTT, DAVID
P SENSENBRENNER
P SERRANO
P SESSIONS
P SEWELL
P SHERMAN
P SHIMKUS
P SHULER
P SHUSTER
P SIMPSON
P SIRES
P SLAUGHTER
P SMITH (NE)
P SMITH (NJ)
P SMITH (TX)
P SMITH (WA)
P SOUTHERLAND
P SPEIER
P STARK
P STEARNS
P STIVERS
P STUTZMAN
SULLIVAN
P SUTTON
P TERRY
P THOMPSON (CA)
P THOMPSON (MS)
P THOMPSON (PA)
P THORNBERRY
P TIBERI
P TIERNEY
P TIPTON
P TONKO
P TOWNS
P TSONGAS
P TURNER
P UPTON
P VAN HOLLEN
P VELAZQUEZ
P VISCLOSKY
P WALBERG
P WALDEN
P WALSH (IL)
P WALZ (MN)
P WASSERMAN SCHULTZ
P WATERS
P WATT
P WAXMAN
P WEBSTER
P WEINER
P WELCH
P WEST
P WESTMORELAND
P WHITFIELD
P WILSON (FL)
P WILSON (SC)
P WITTMAN
P WOLF
P WOMACK
P WOODALL
P WOOLSEY
P WU
P YARMUTH
P YODER
P YOUNG (AK)
P YOUNG (FL)
P YOUNG (IN)

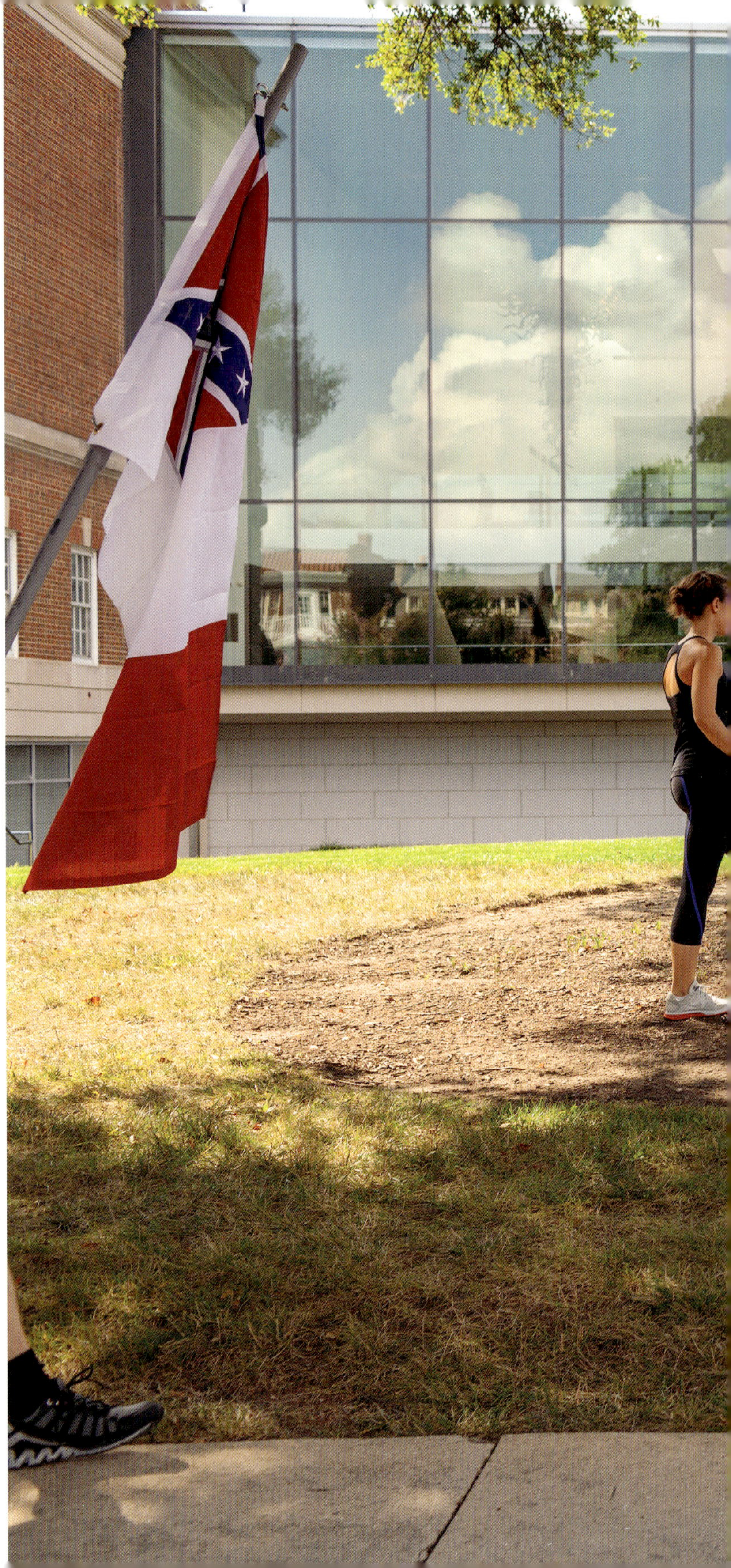

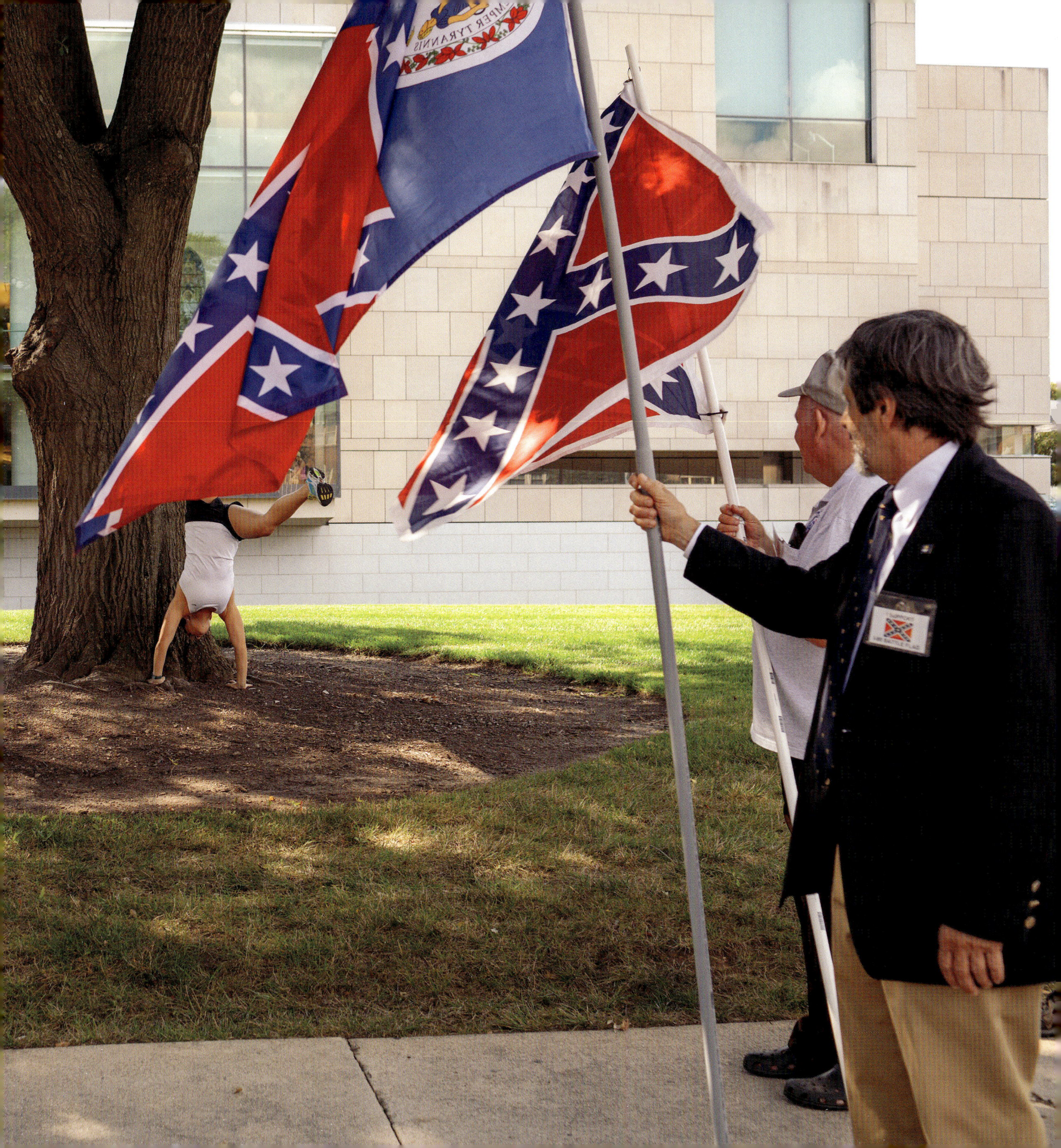
TYRANNIS

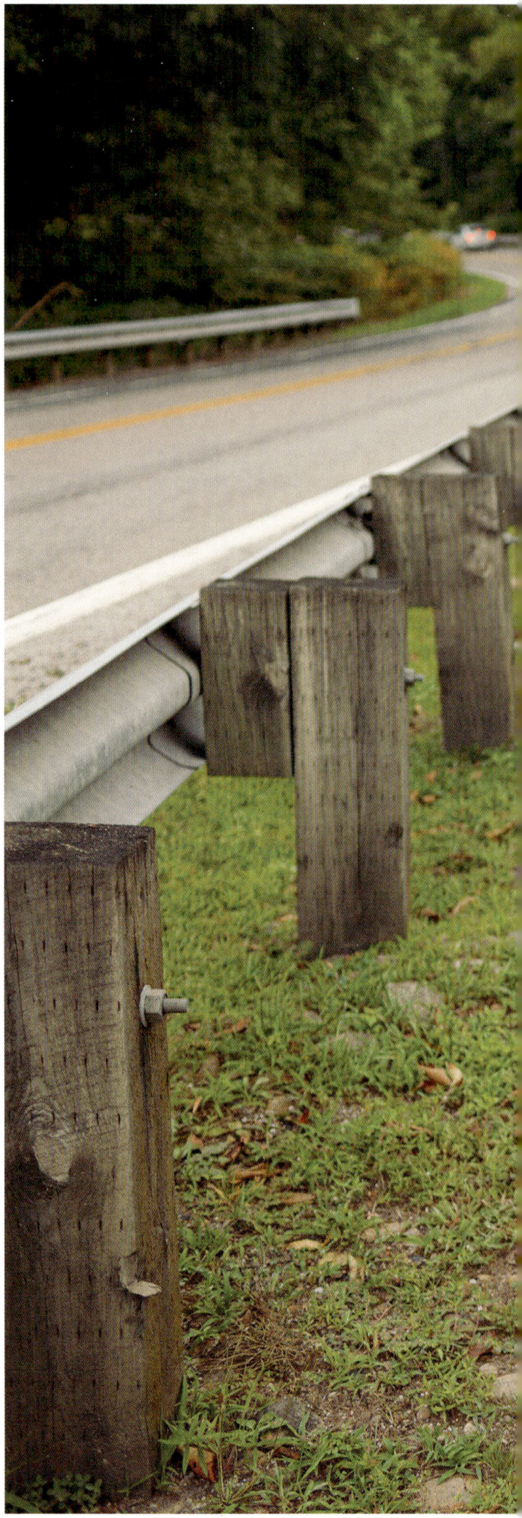

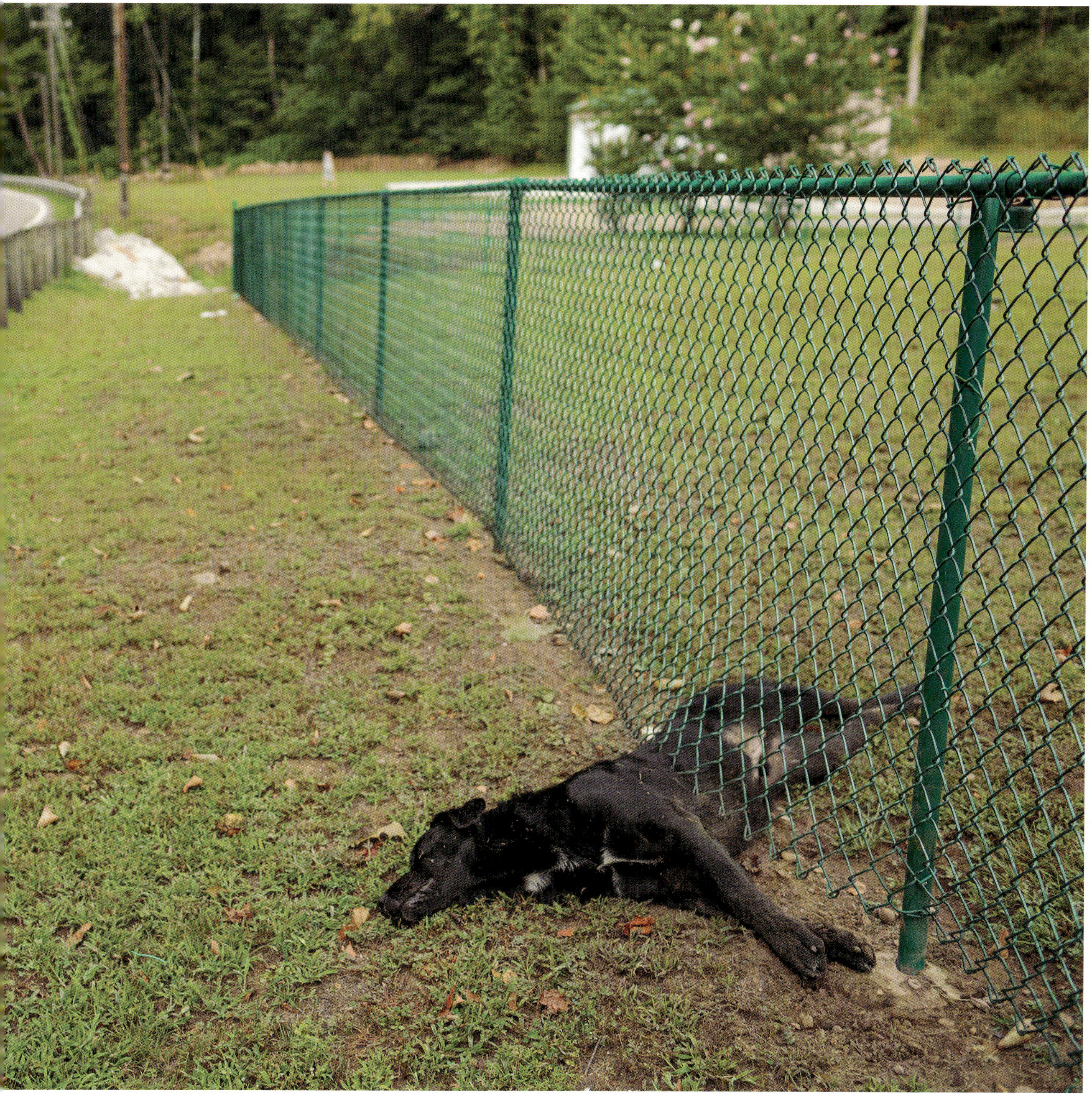

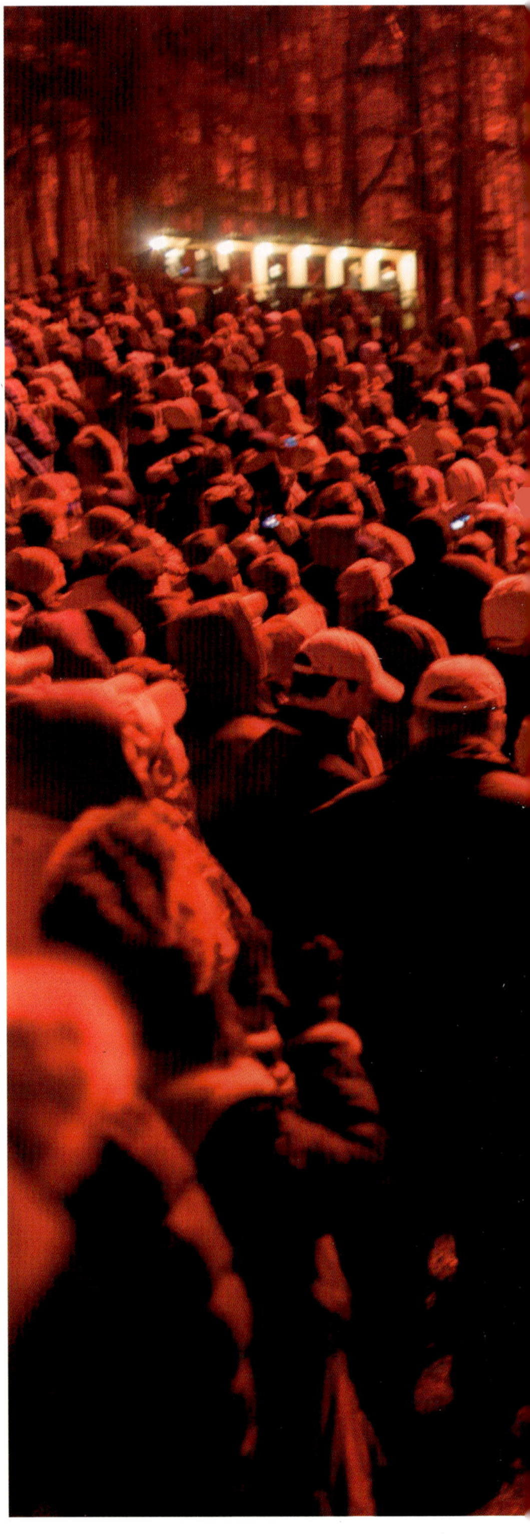

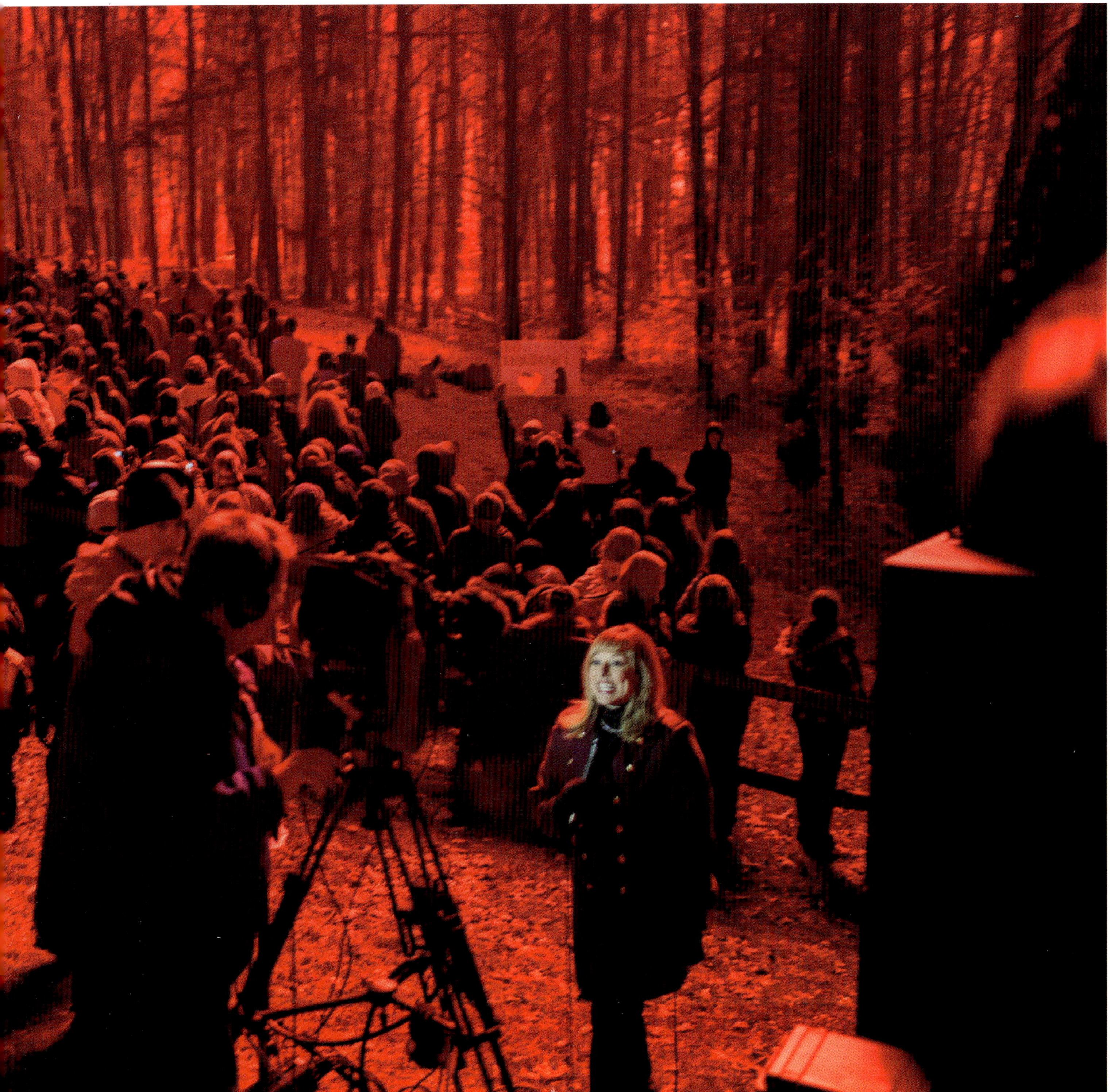

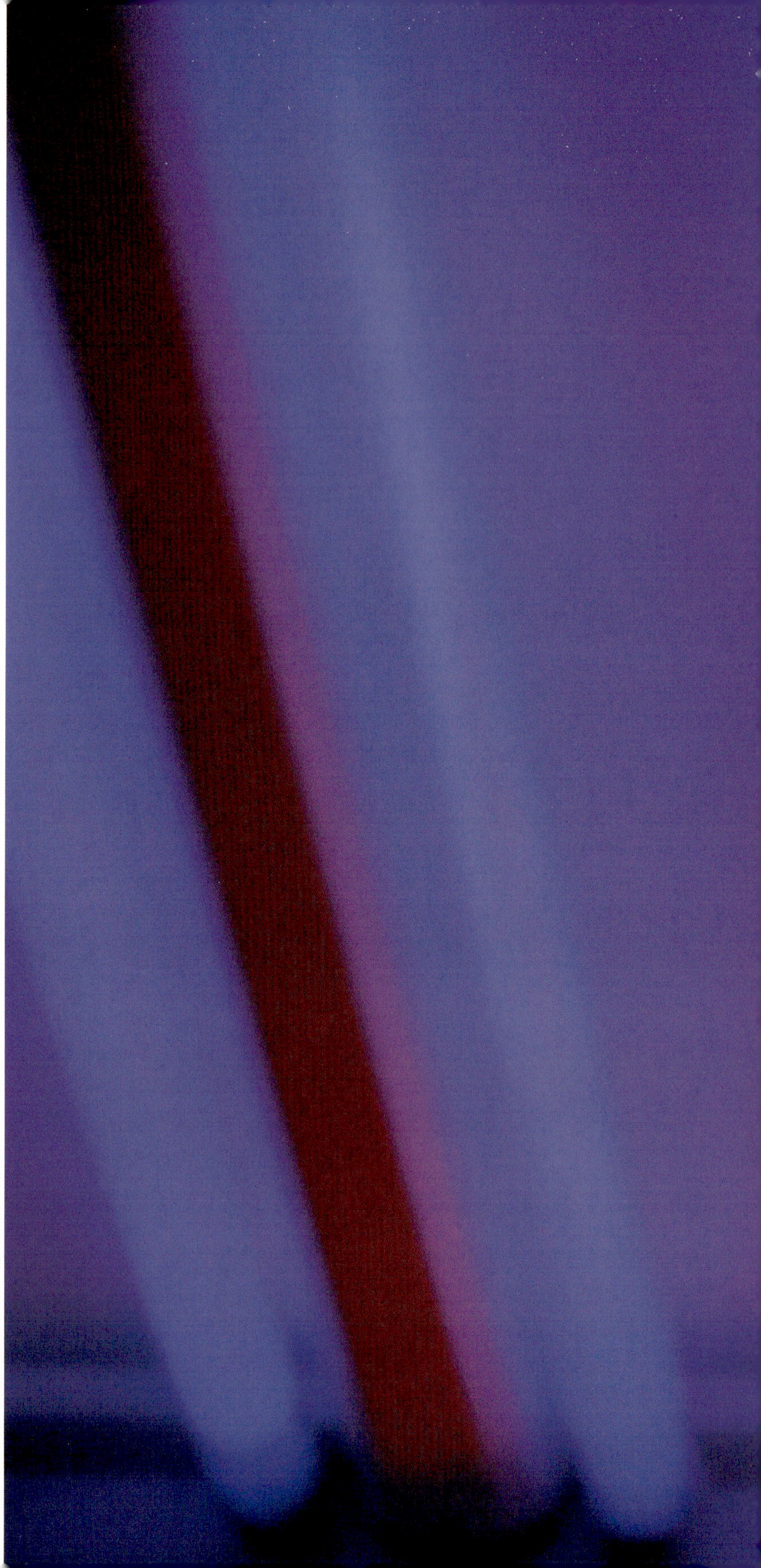

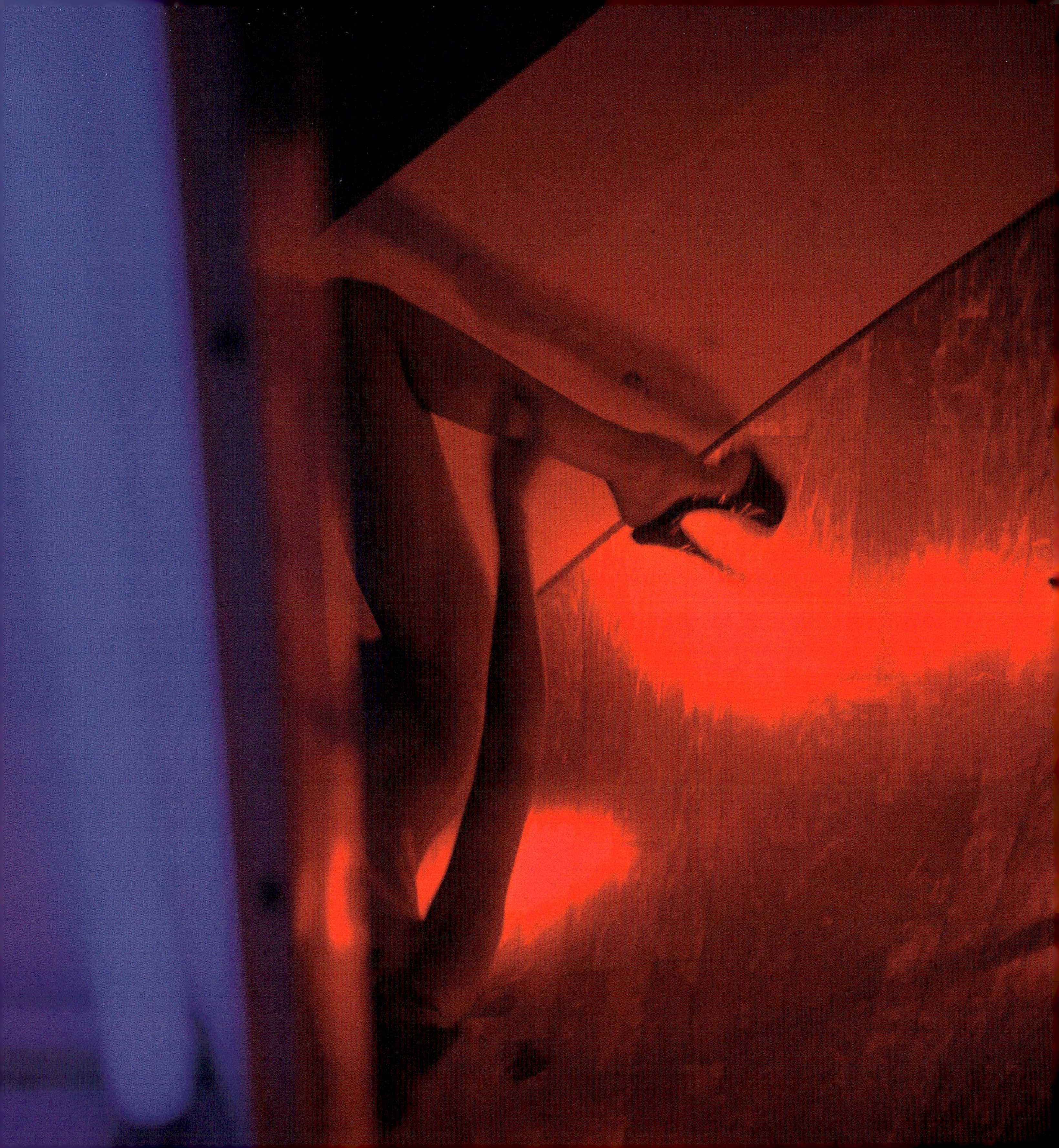

119

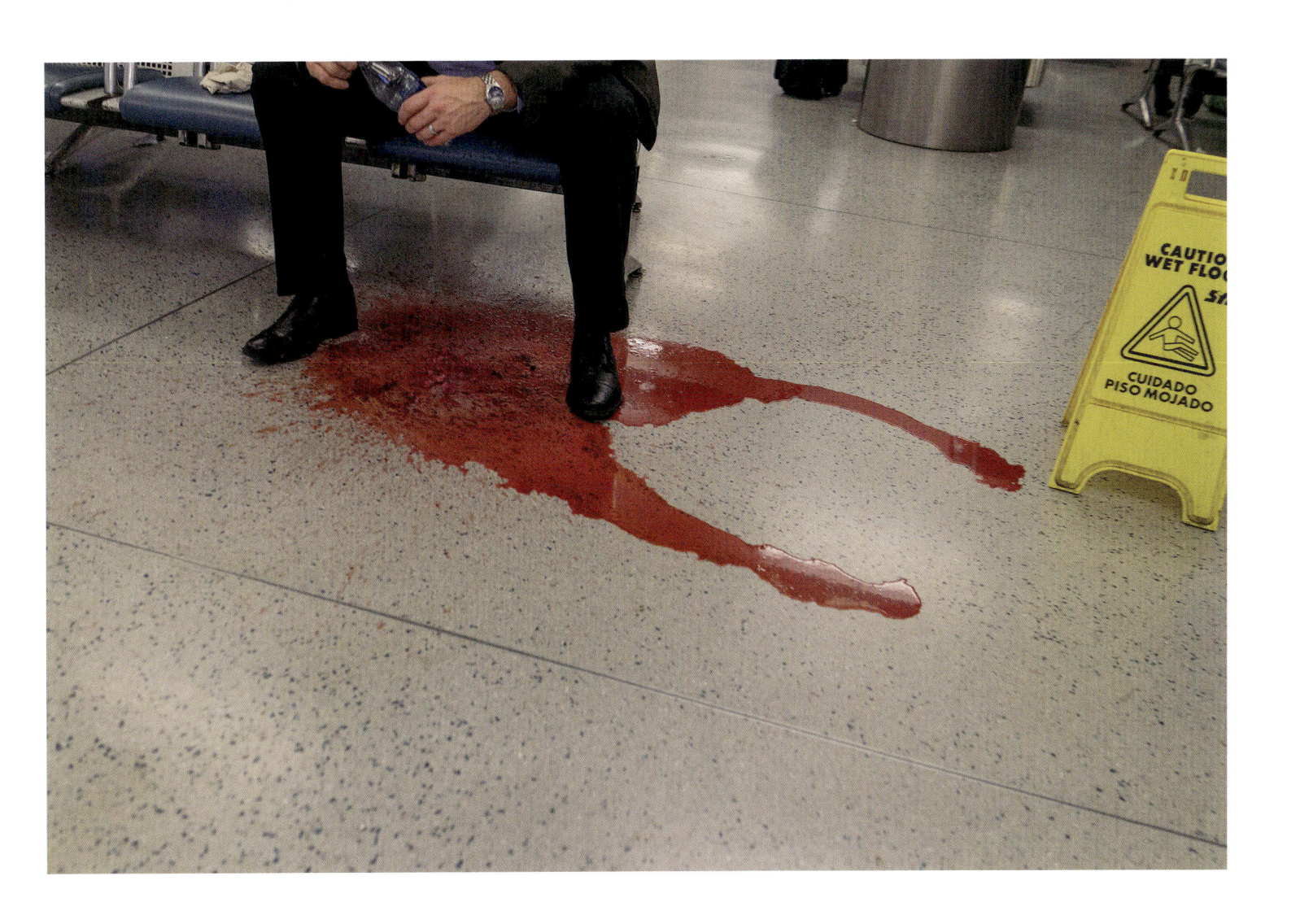

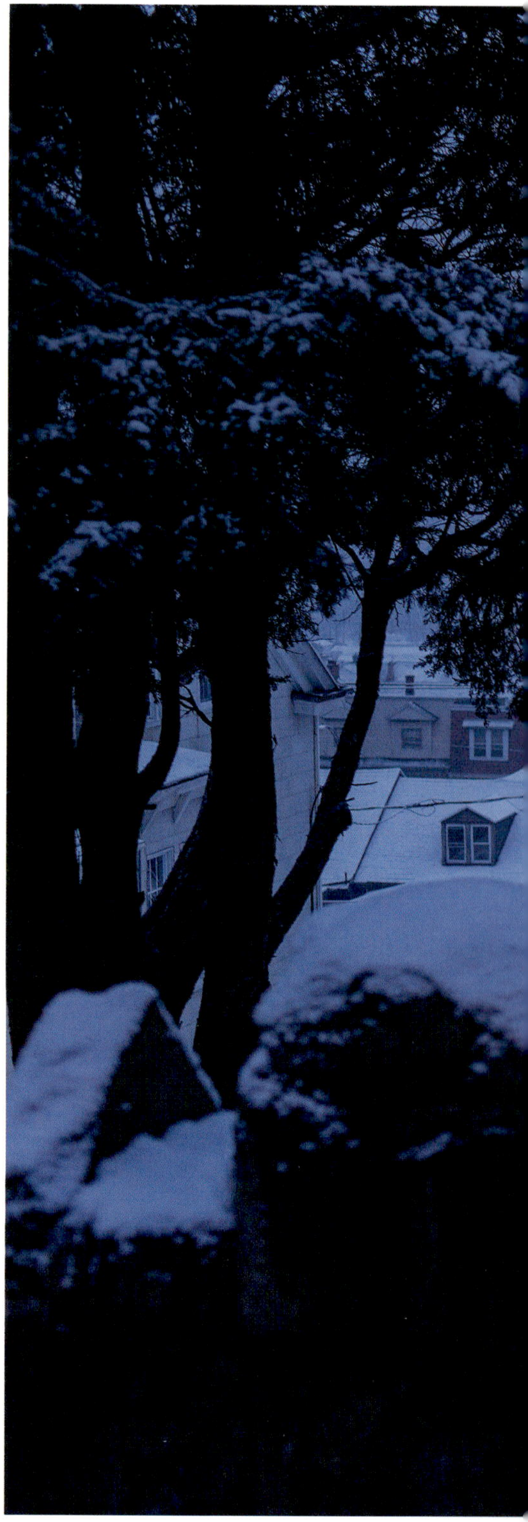

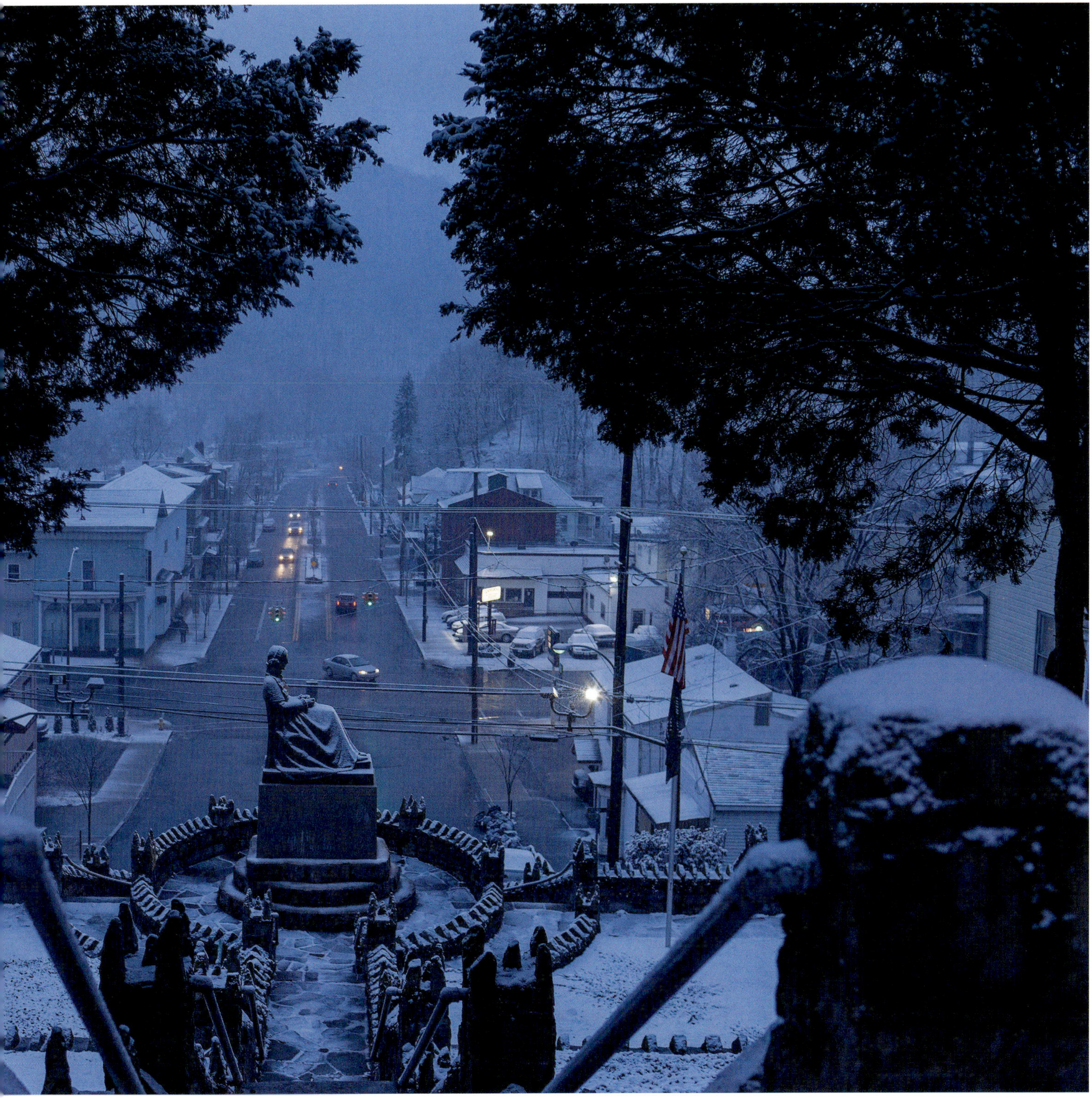

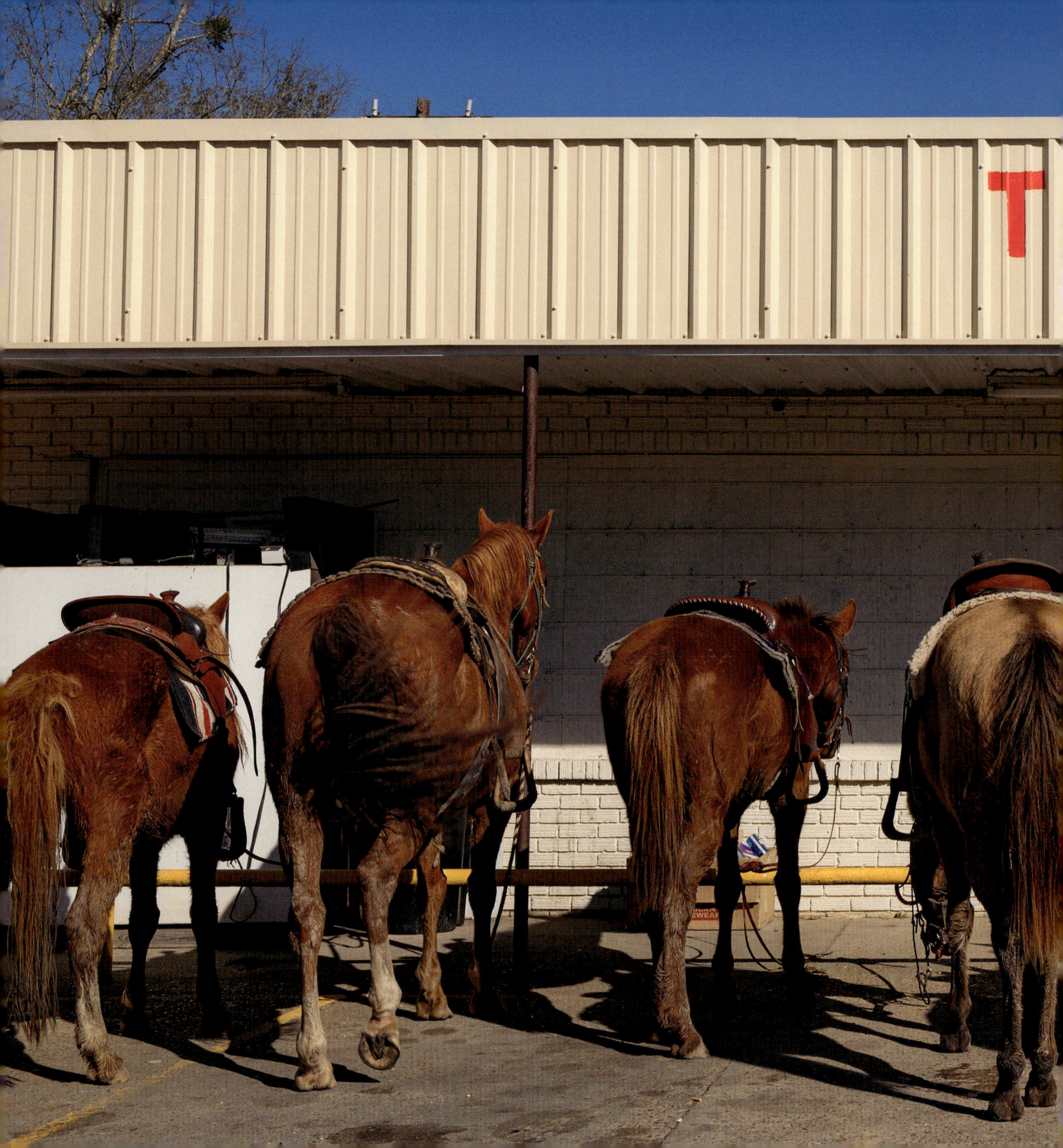

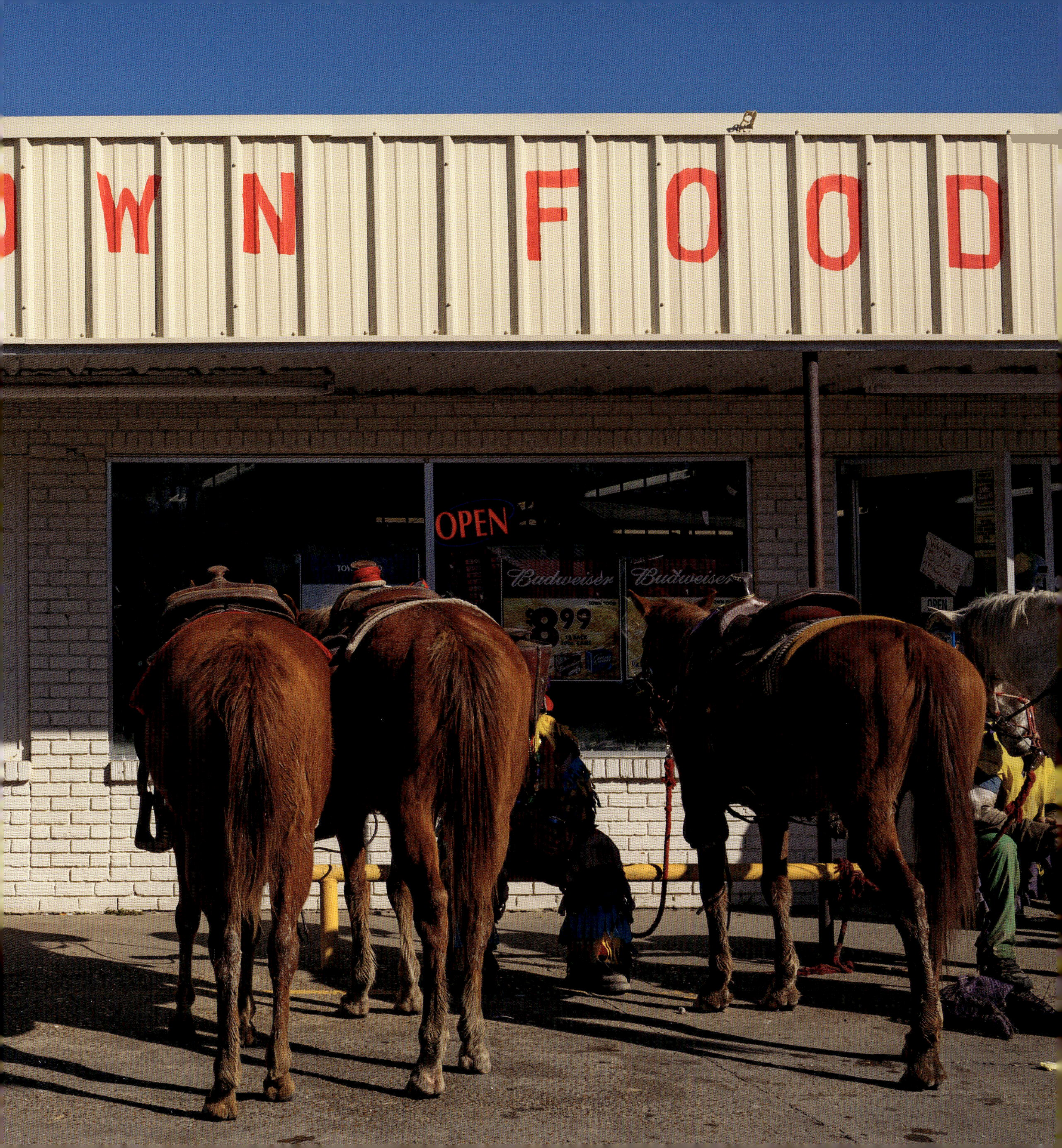
OWN FOOD
OPEN
Budweiser
Budweiser
$8.99

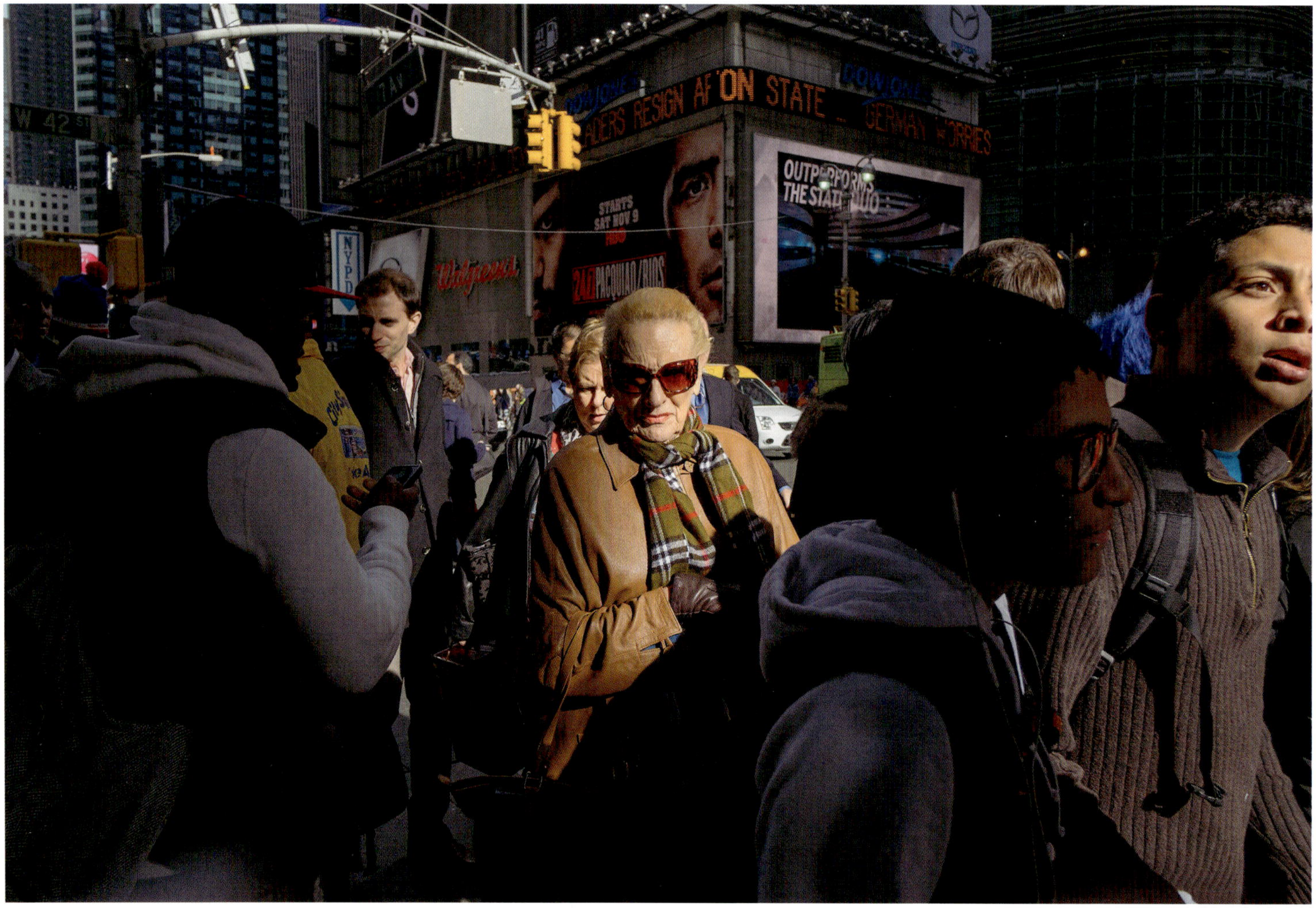
Walgreens
STARTS
SAT NOV 9
PACQUIAO/RIOS
NYPD

125

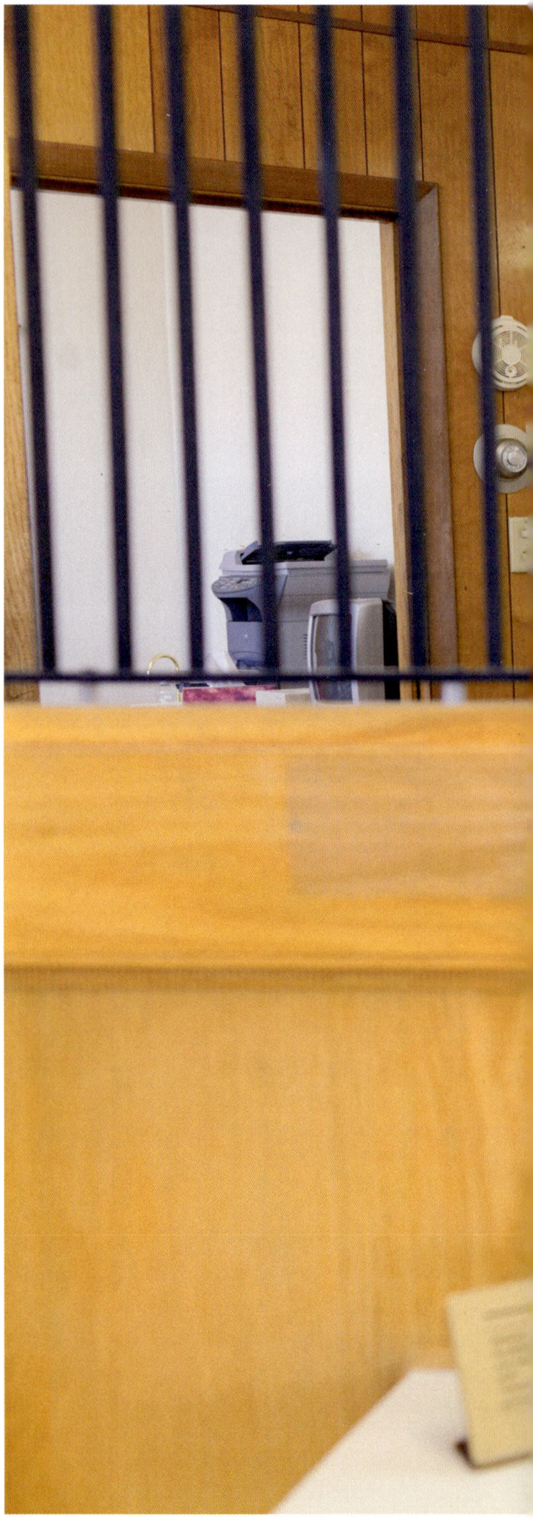

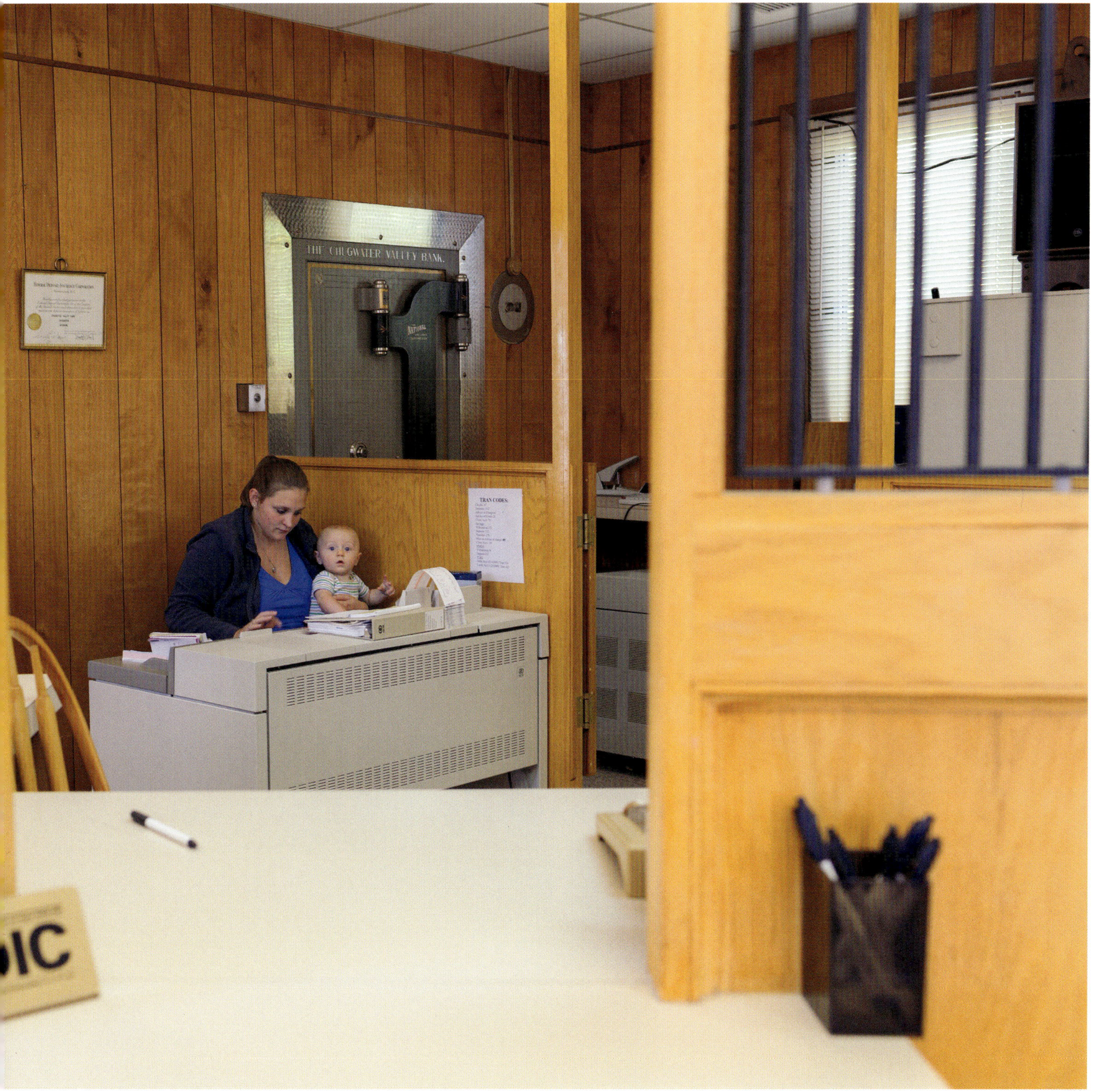
THE CHUGWATER VALLEY BANK
TRAN CODES:

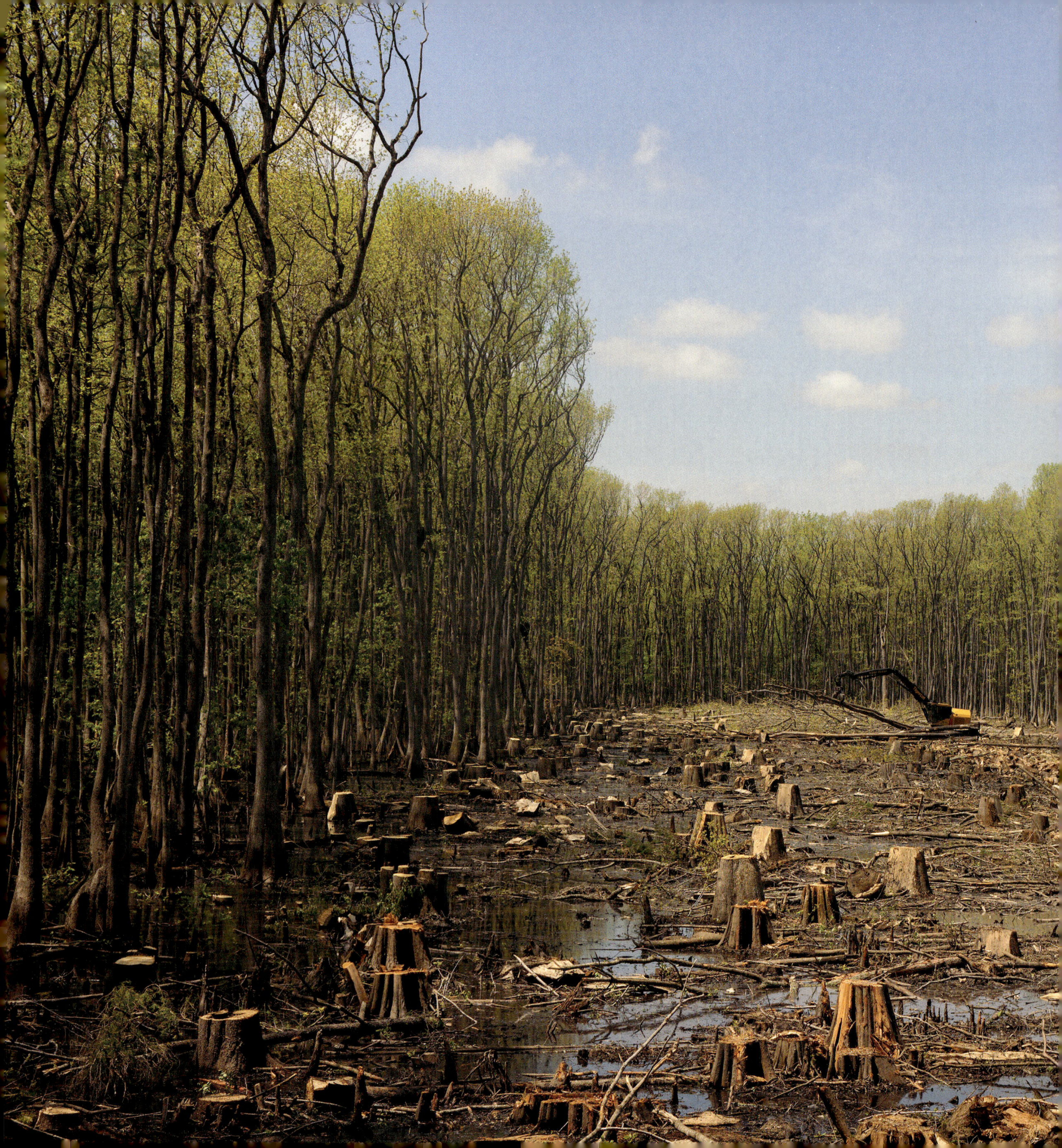

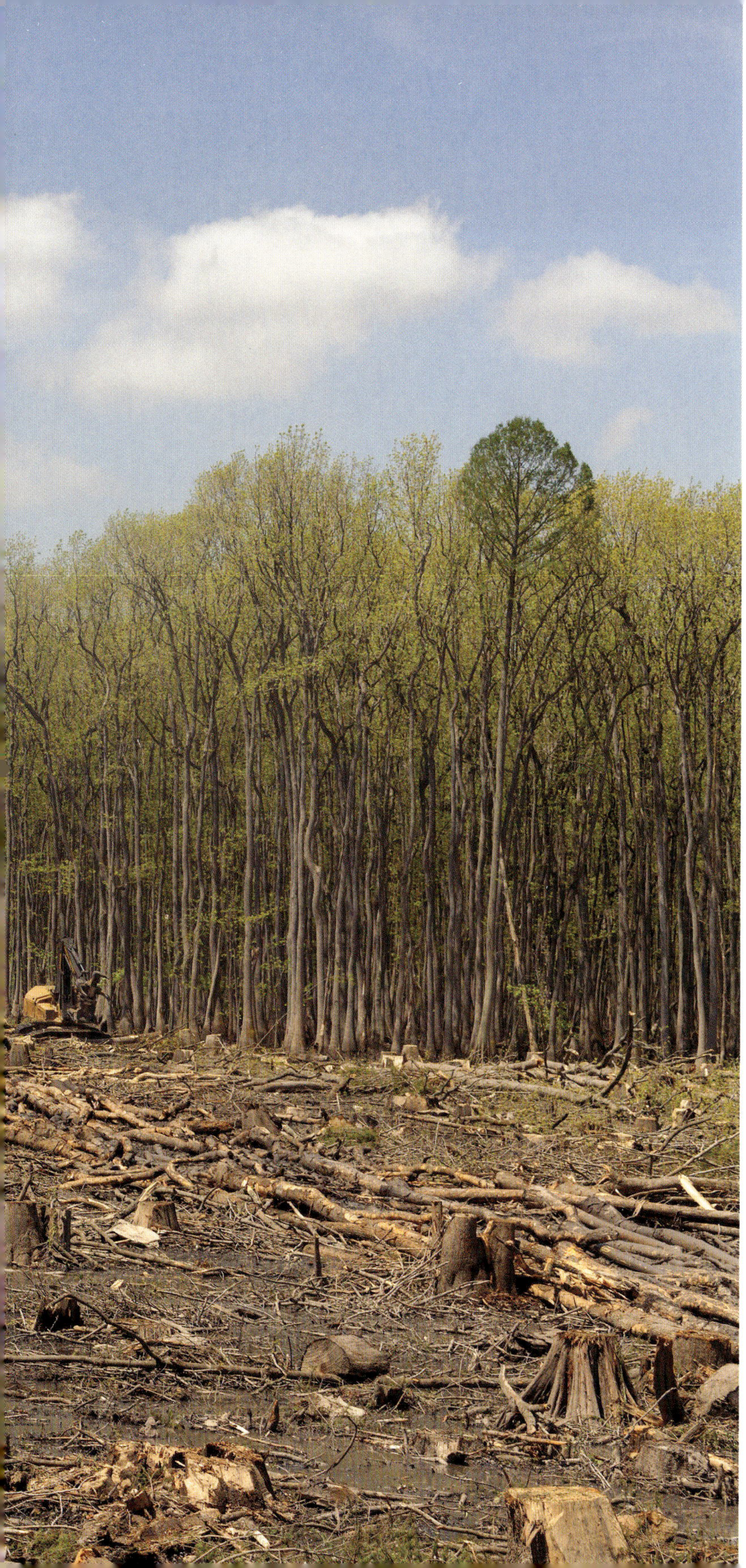

Amazing Grace
LYRICS: Fanny Jane Crosby
MUSIC: William James Kirkpatrick

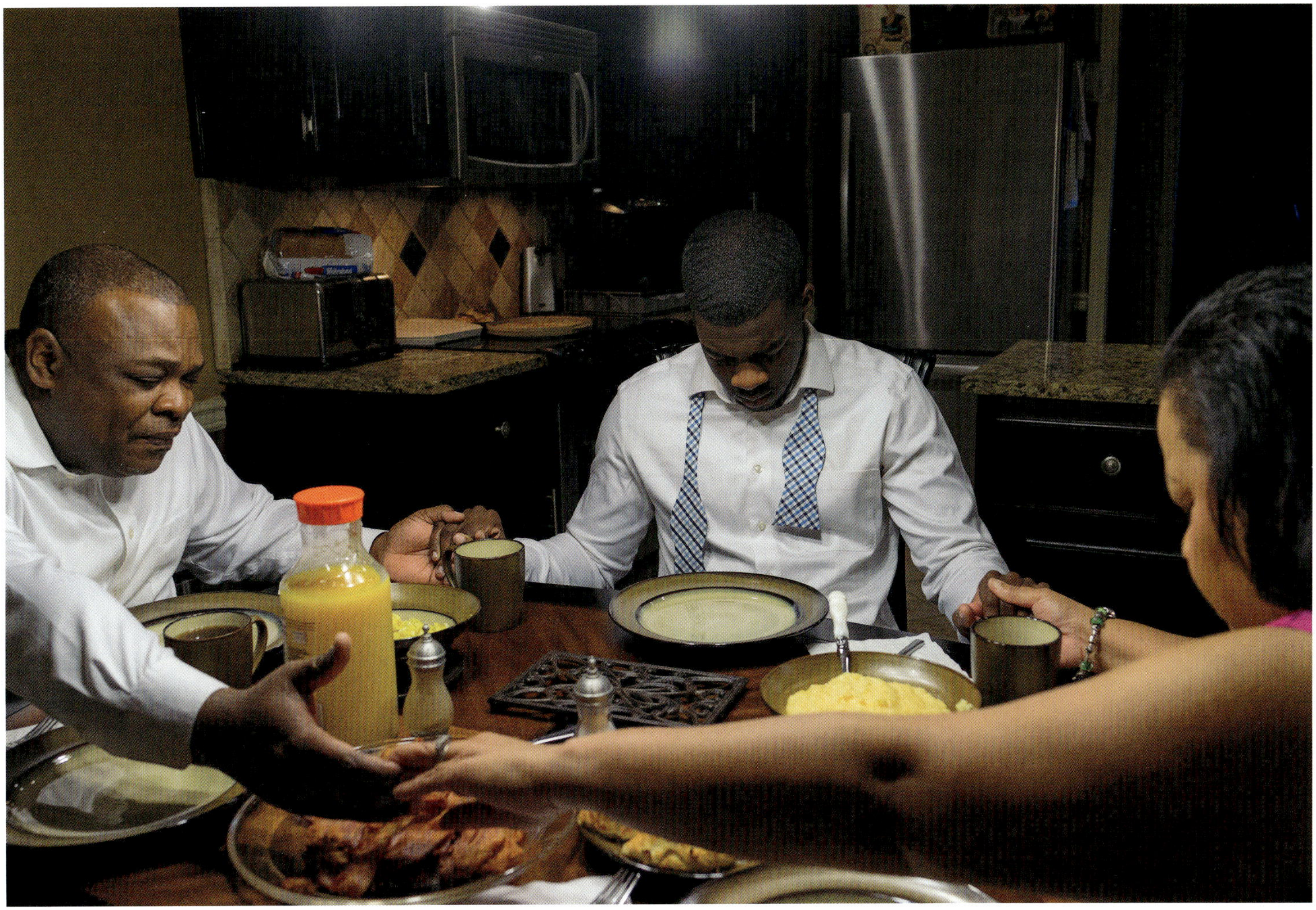

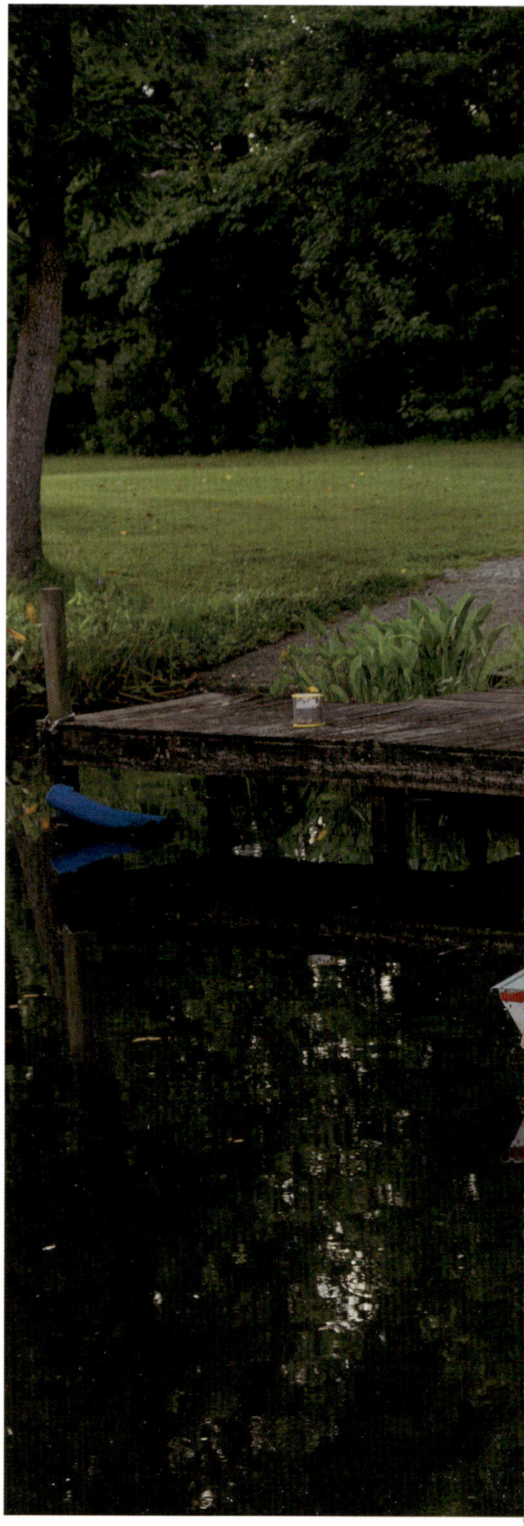

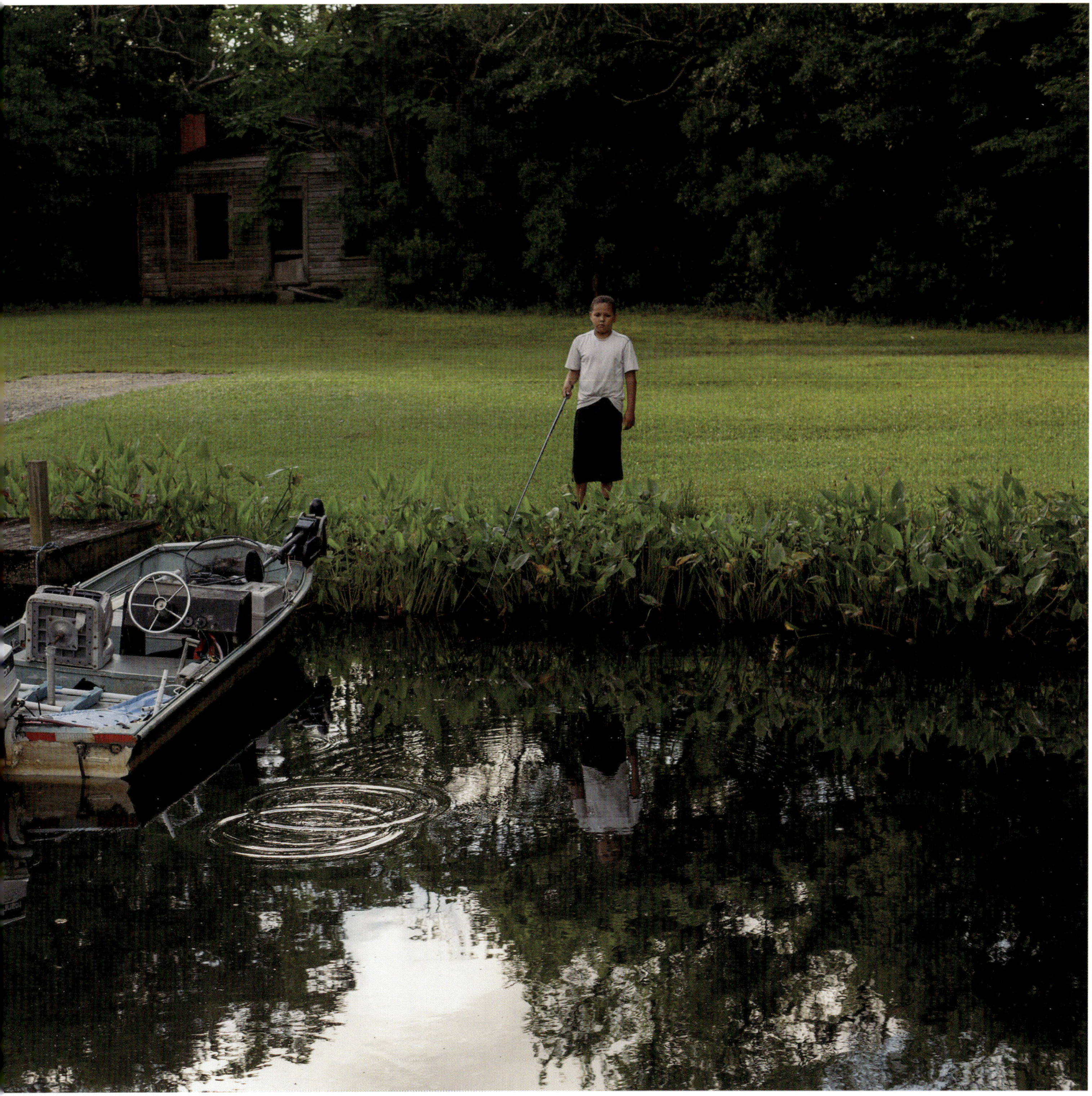

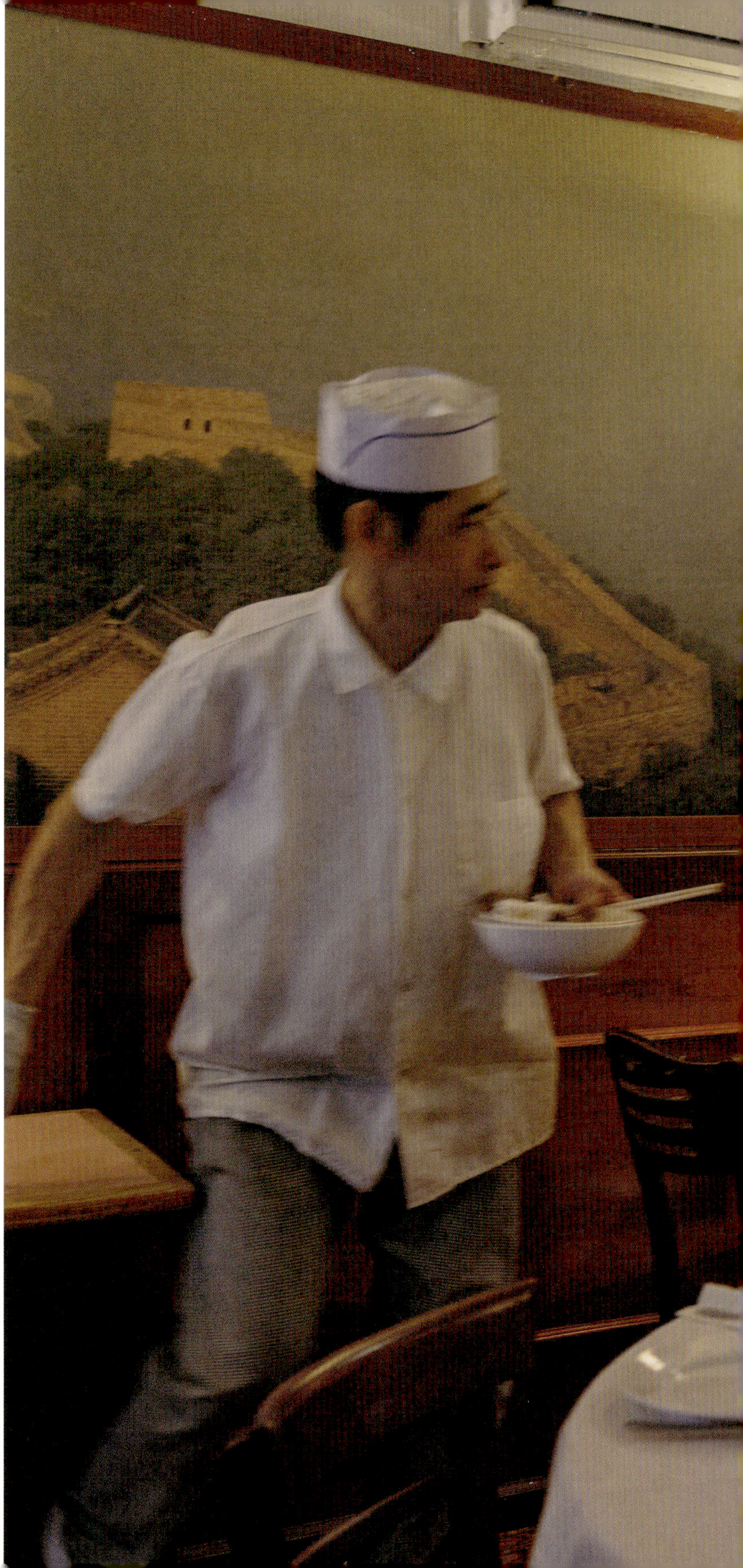

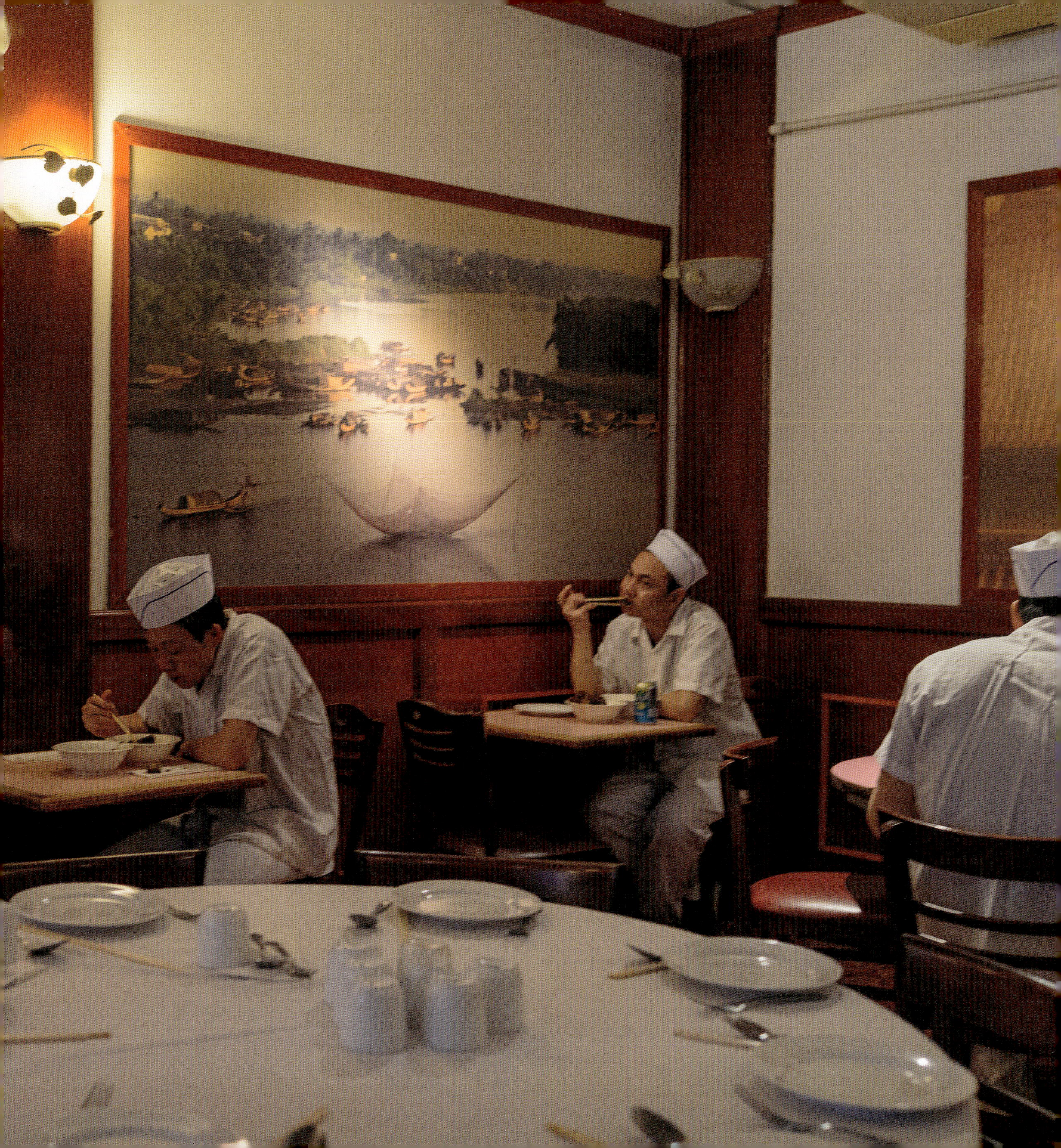

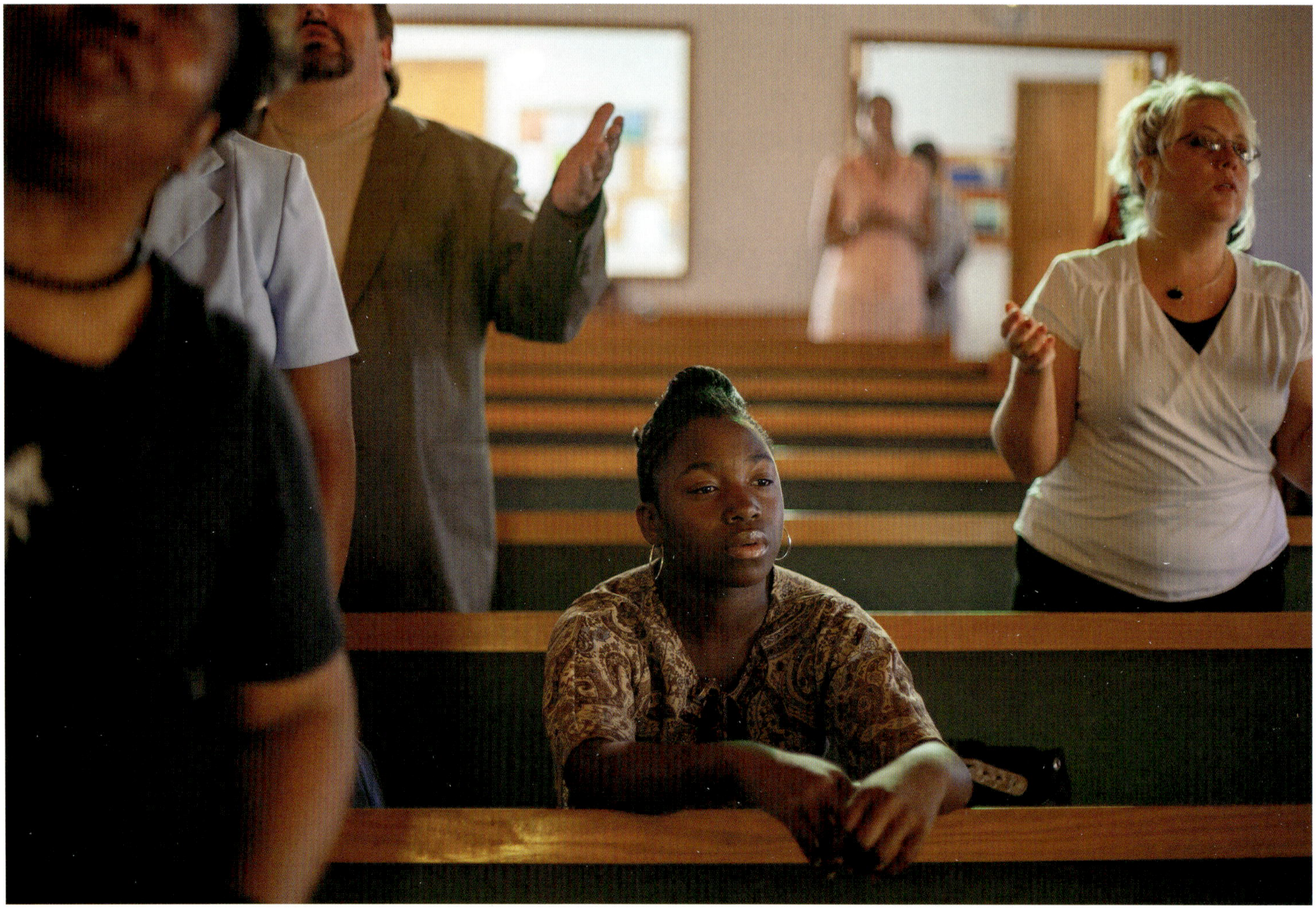

139

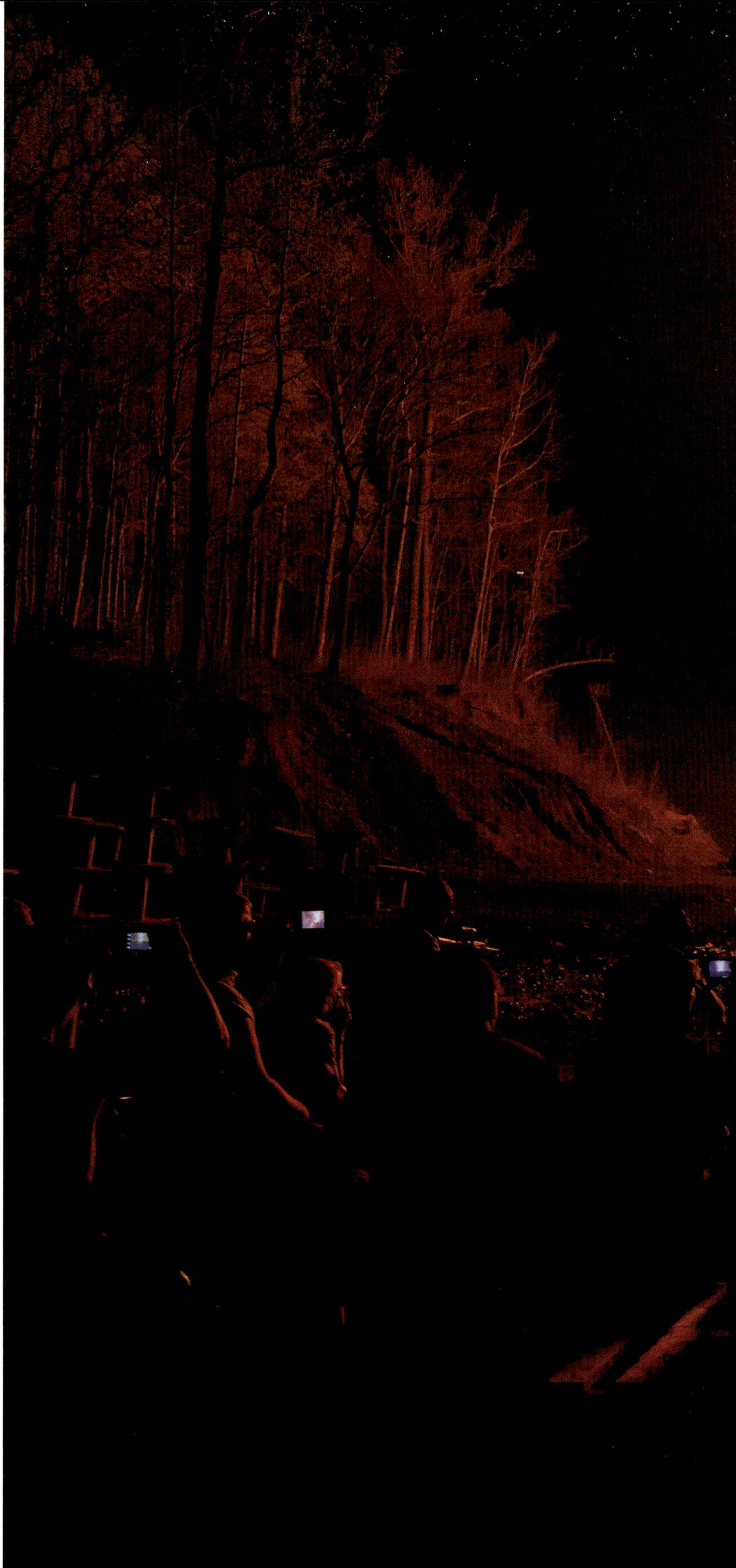

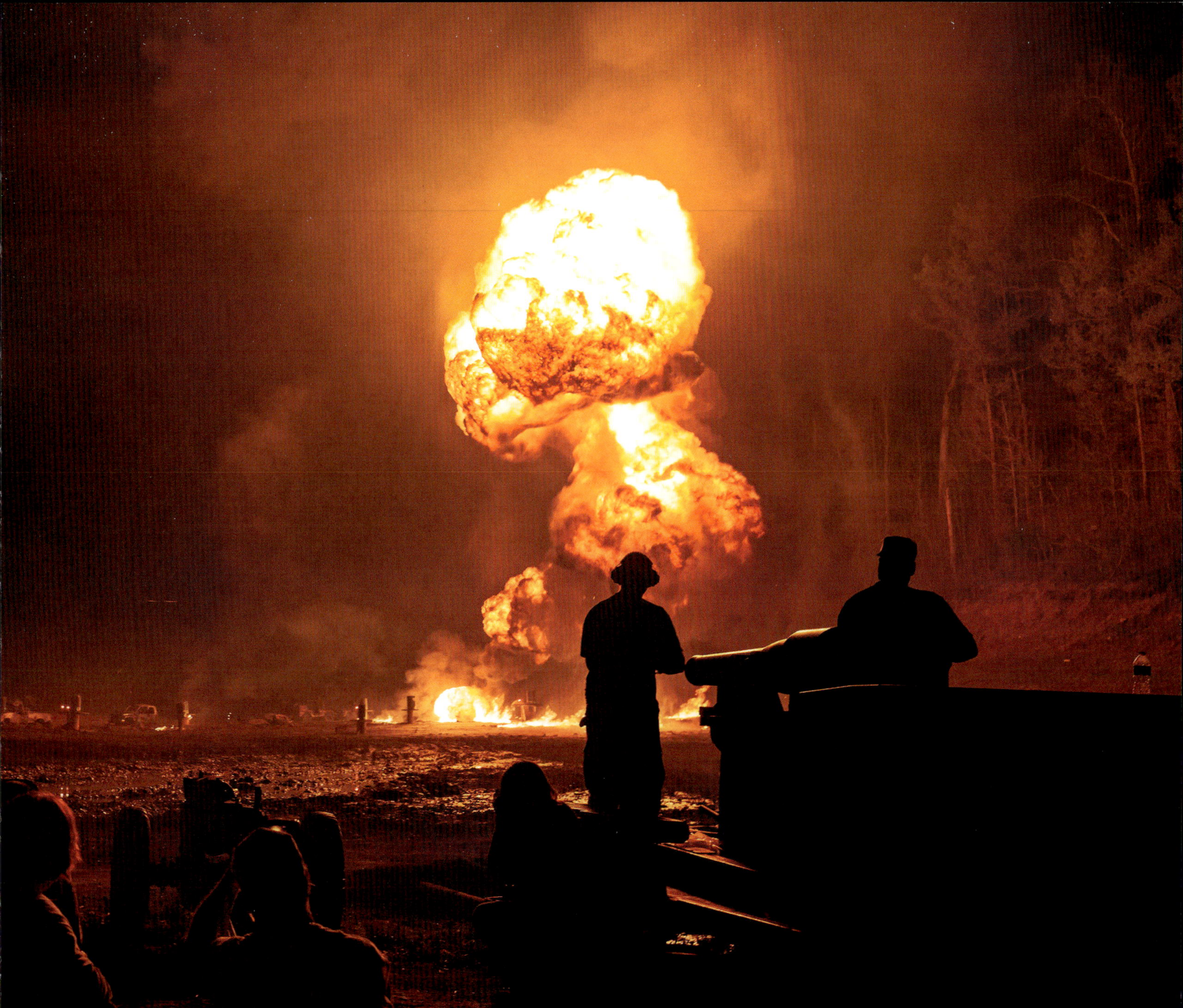

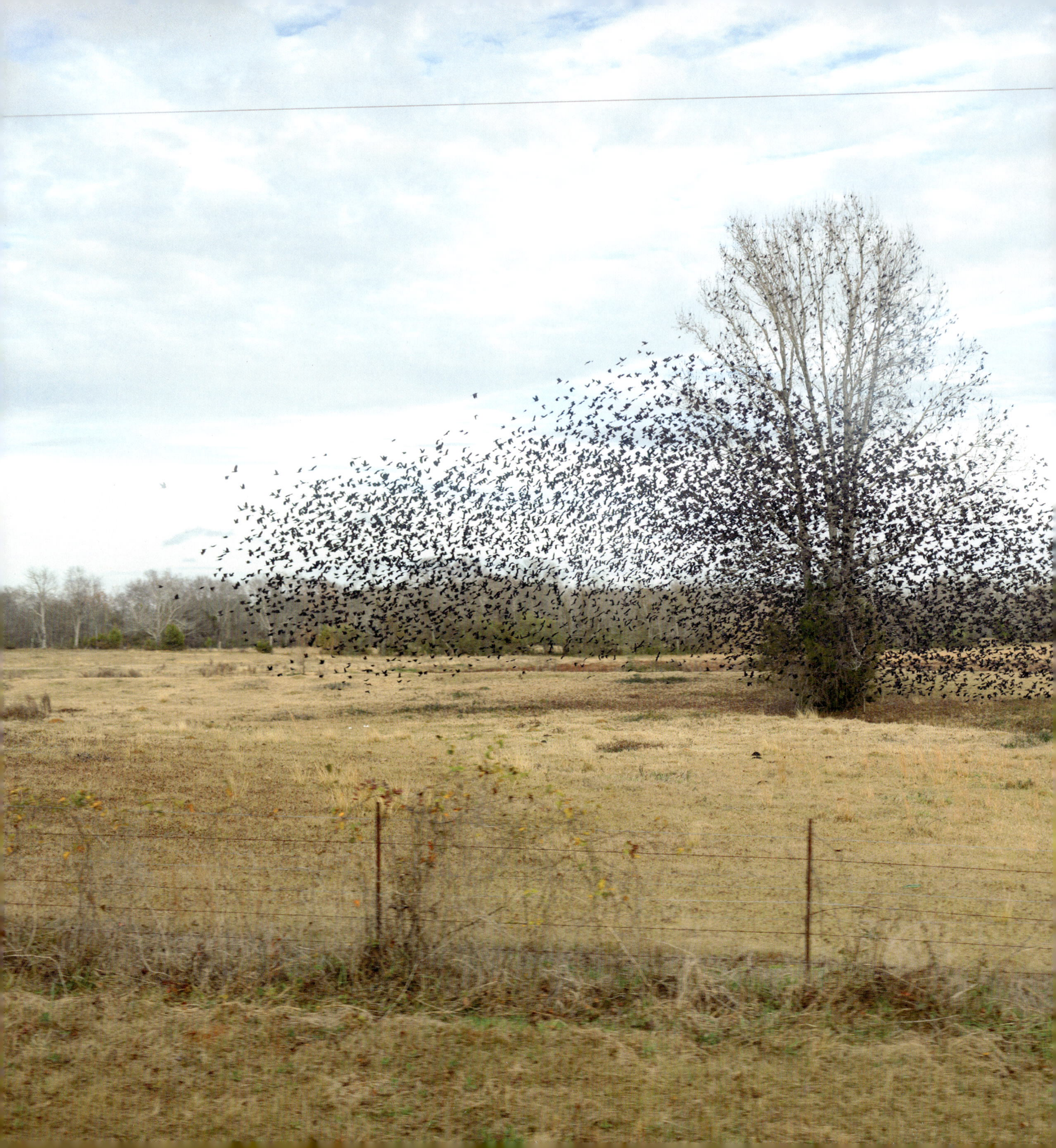

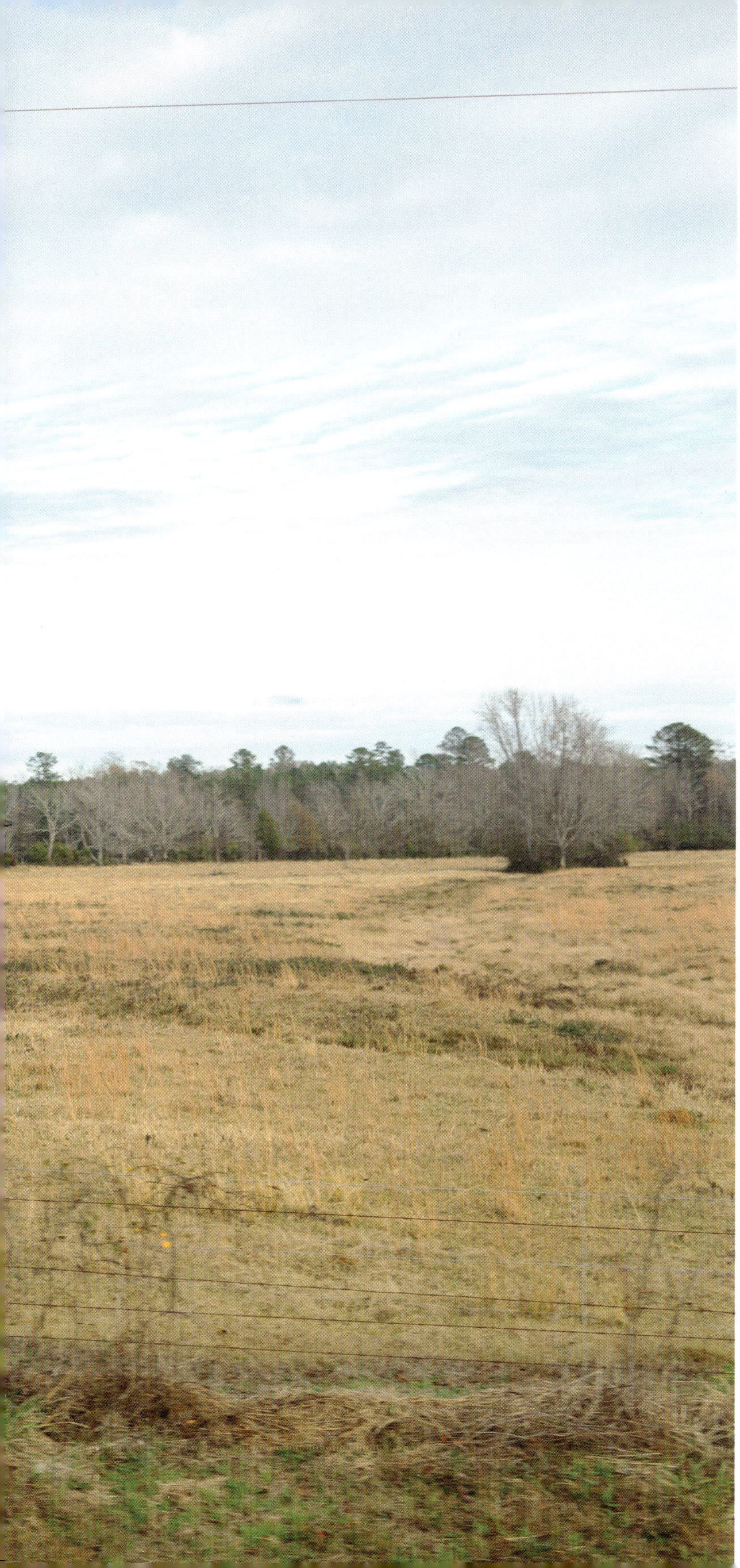

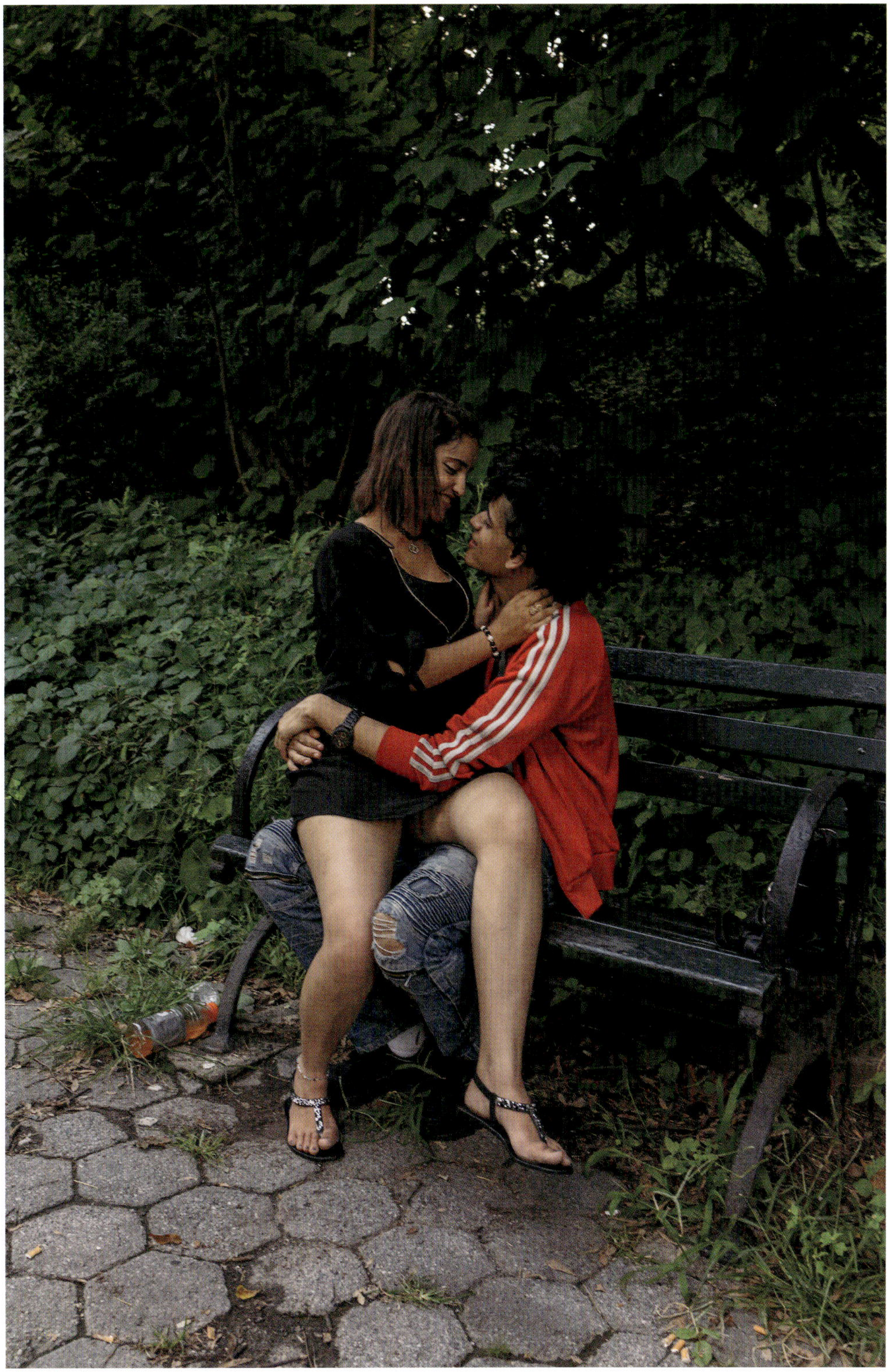

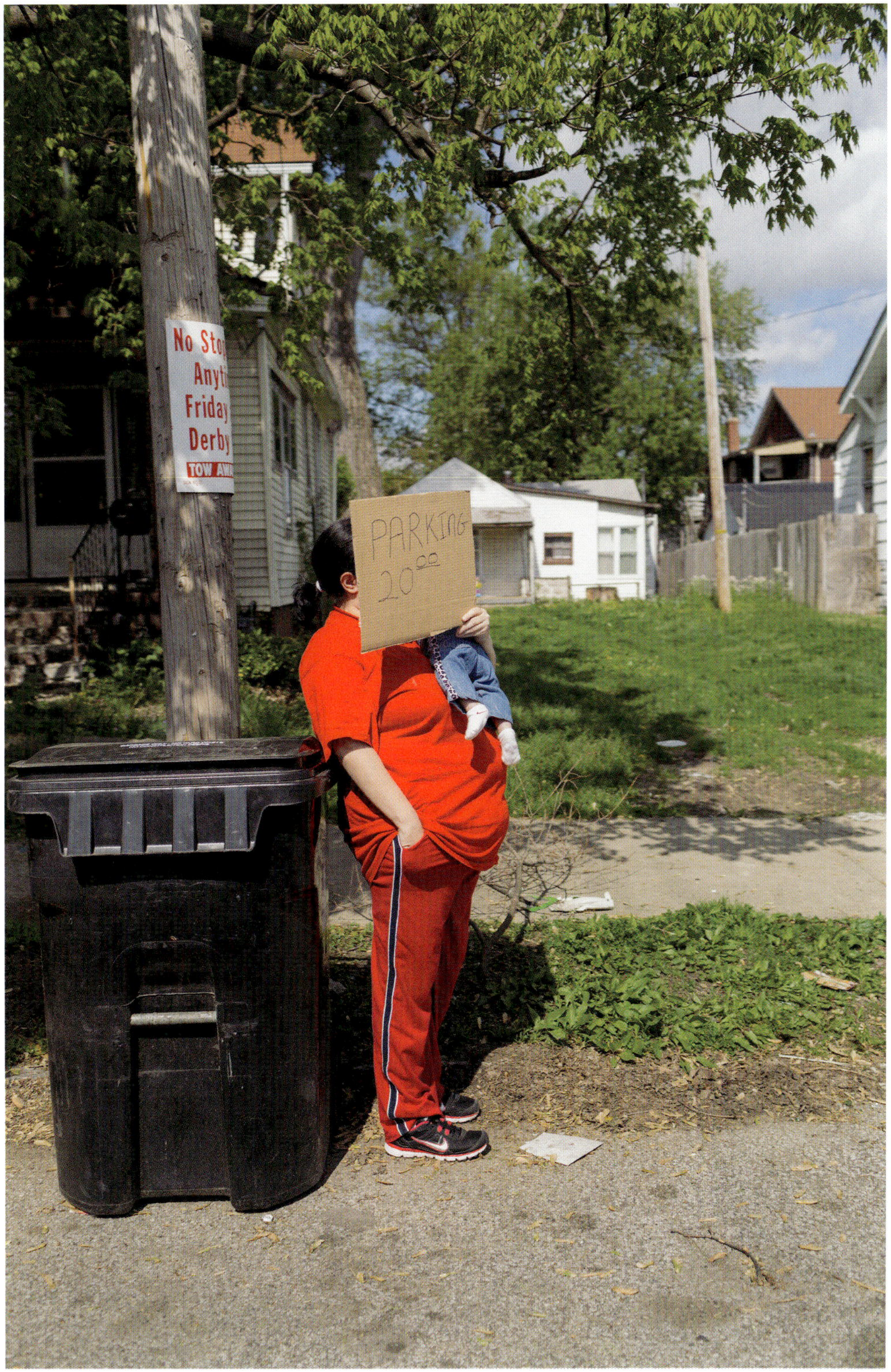
No
Friday
Derby
PARKING
$20^{00}$

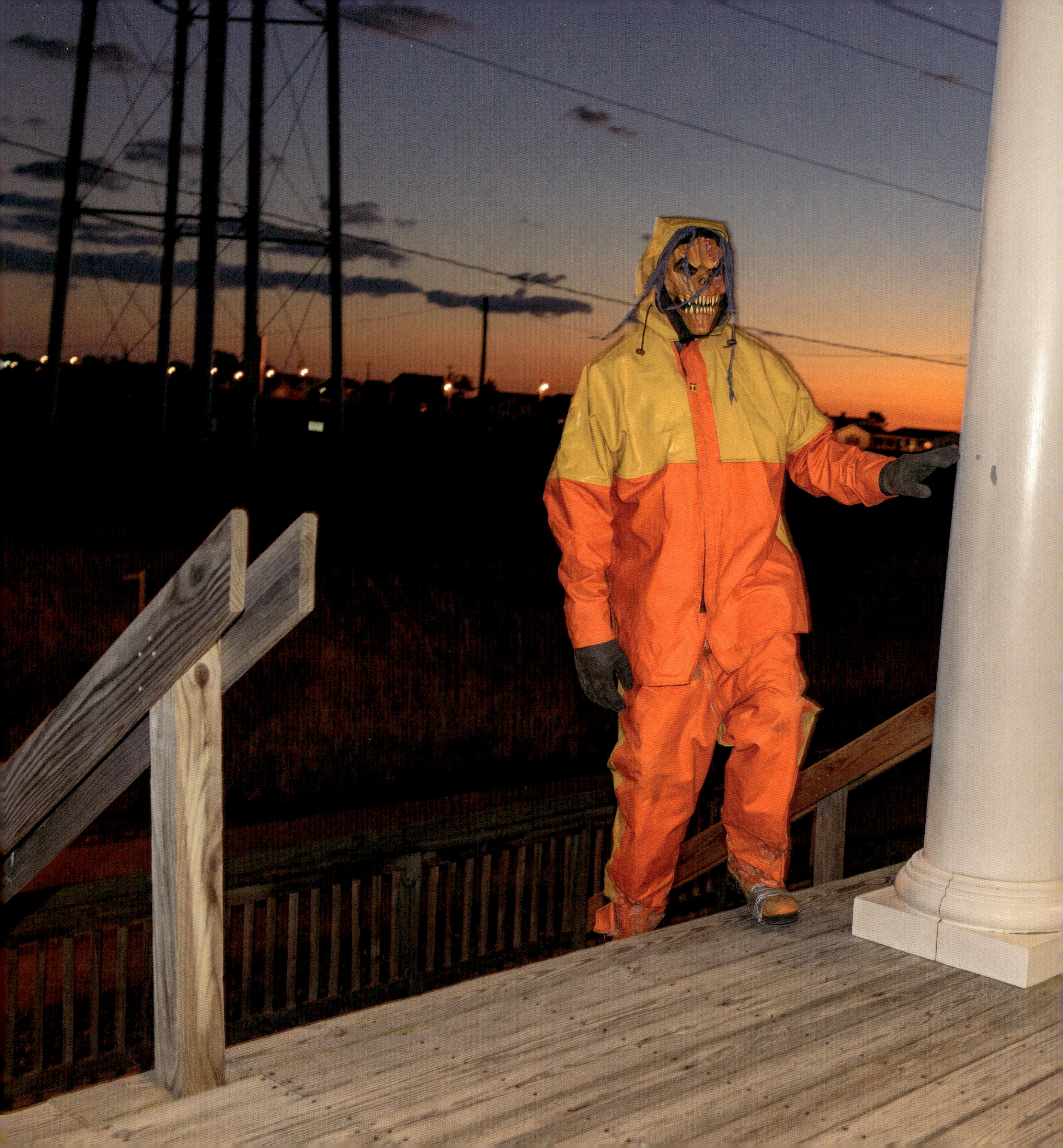

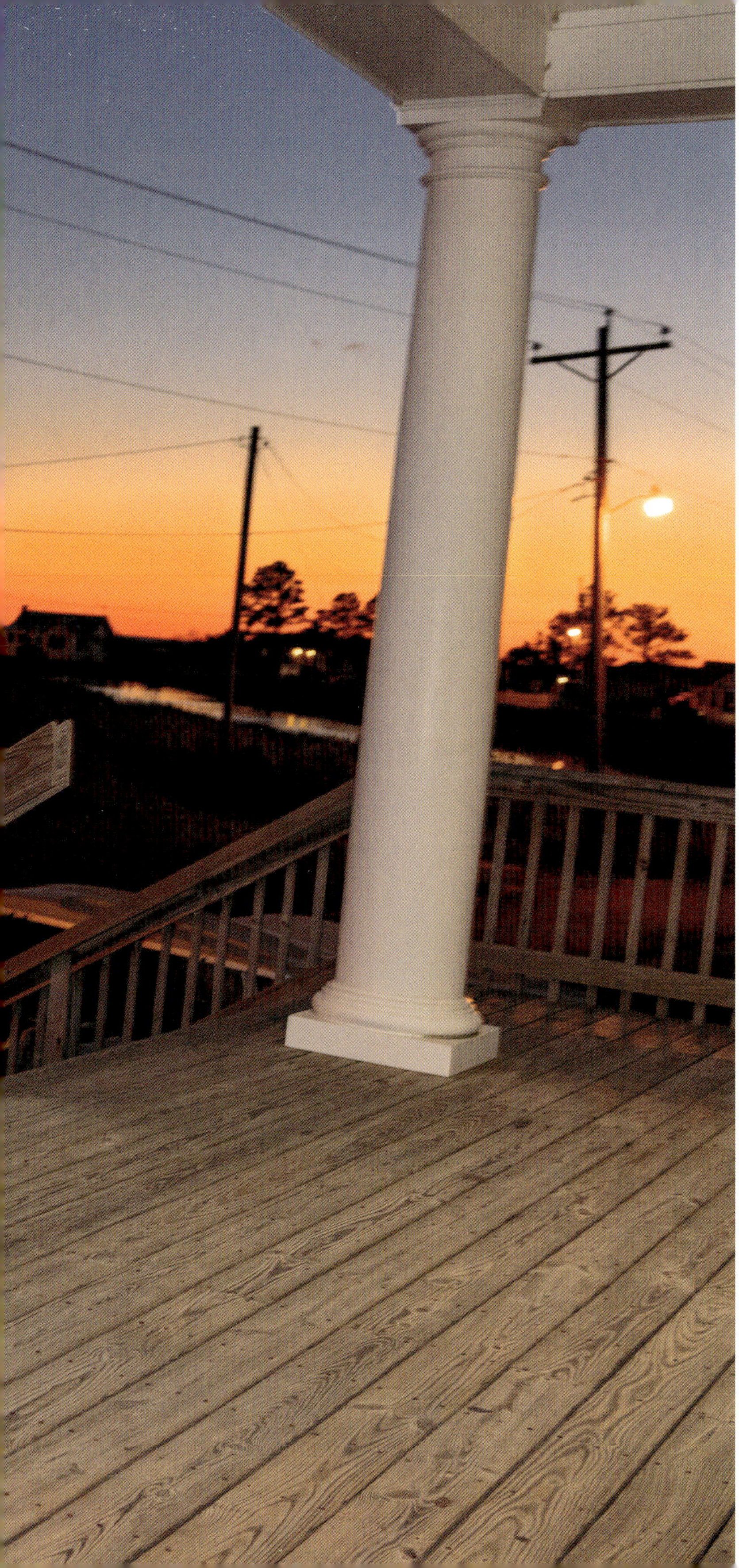

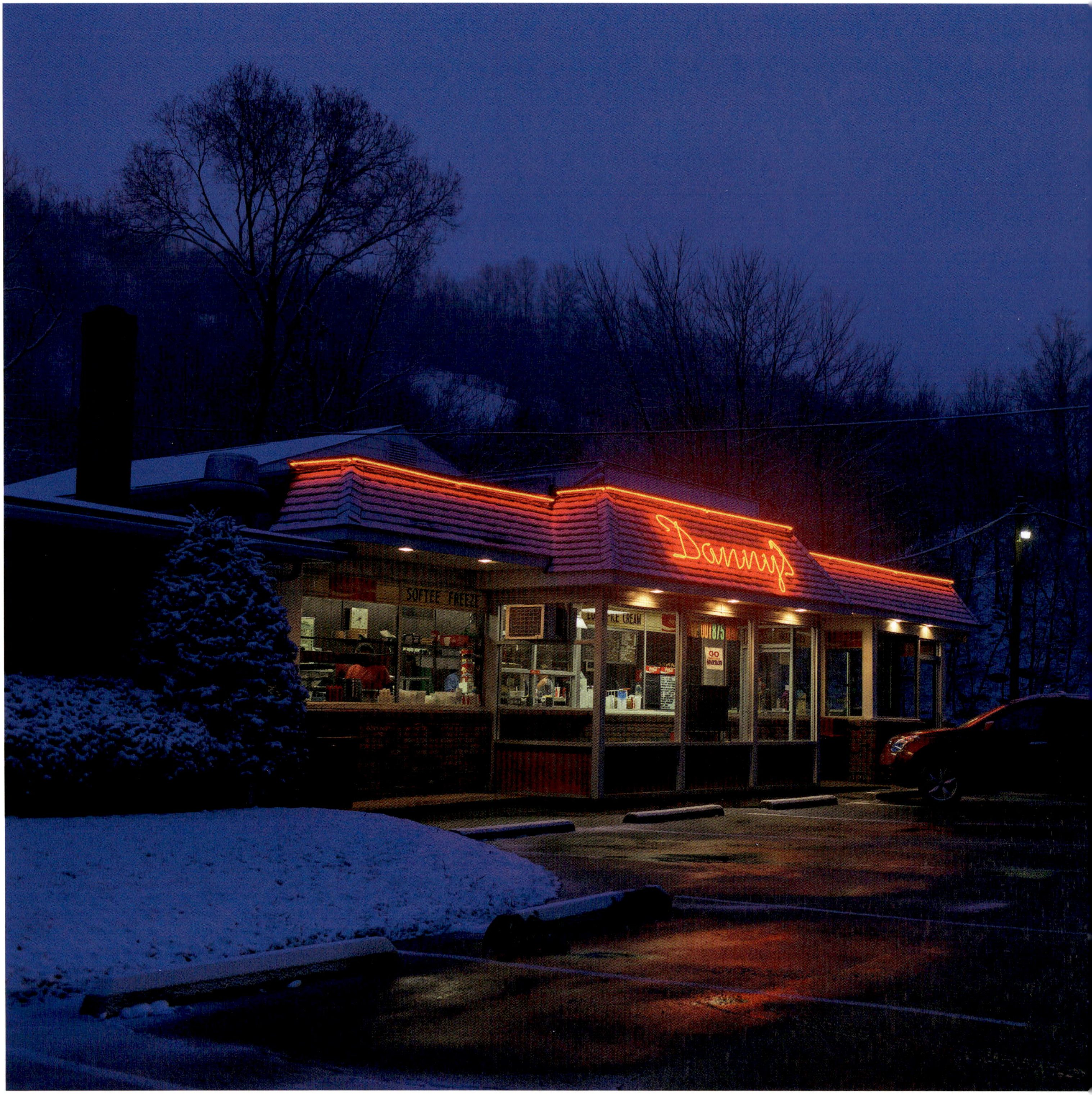
Danny's
SOFTEE FREEZE

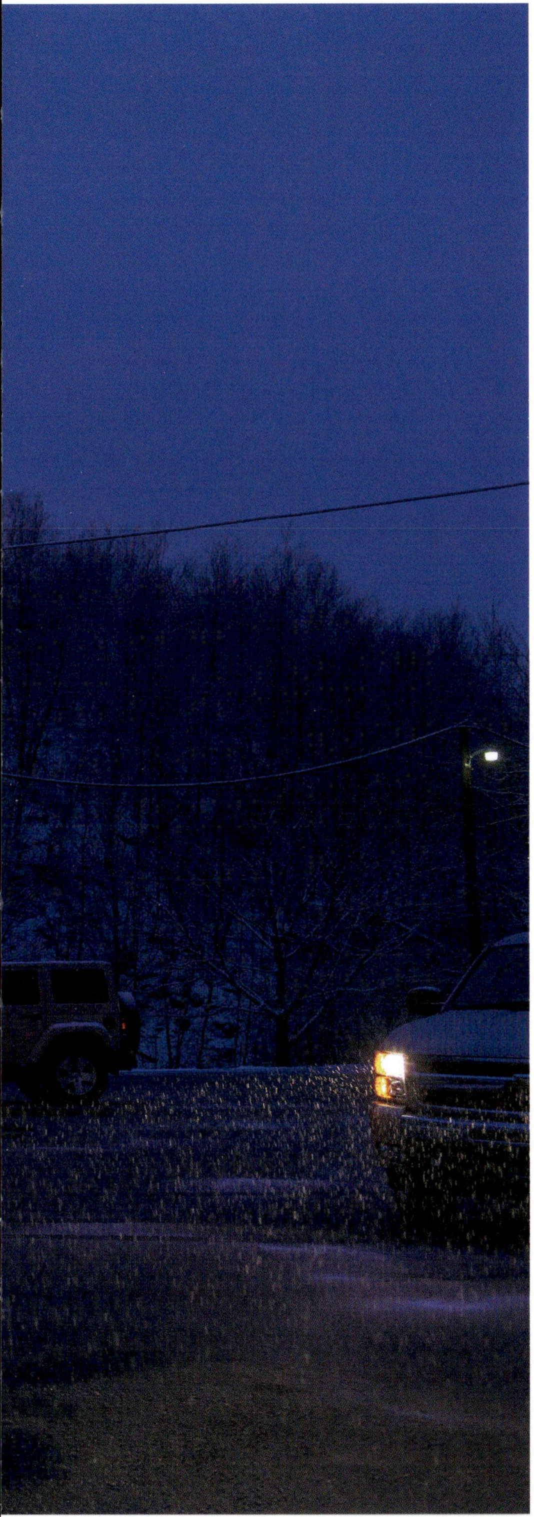

153

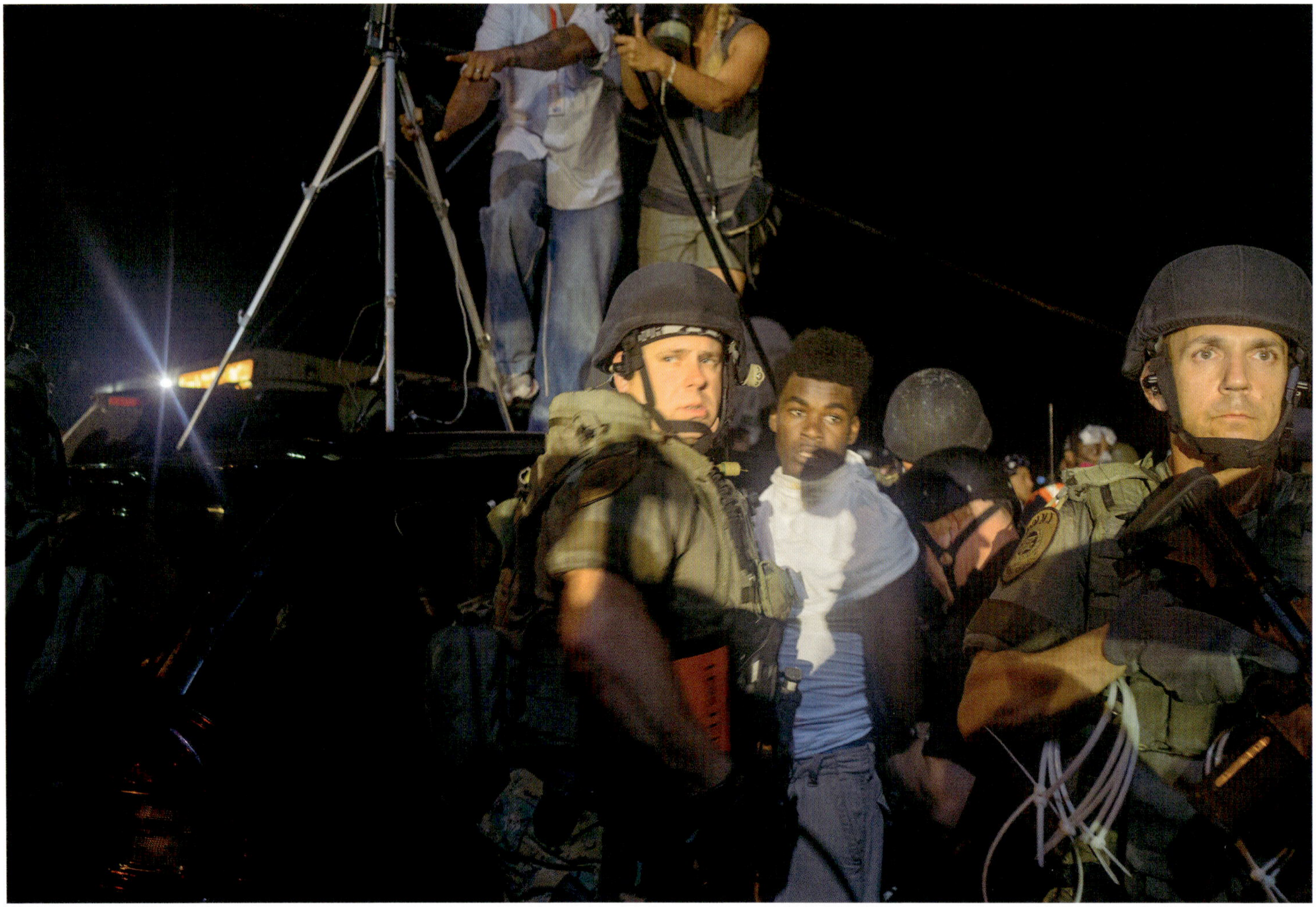

155

156

SKIN SALES

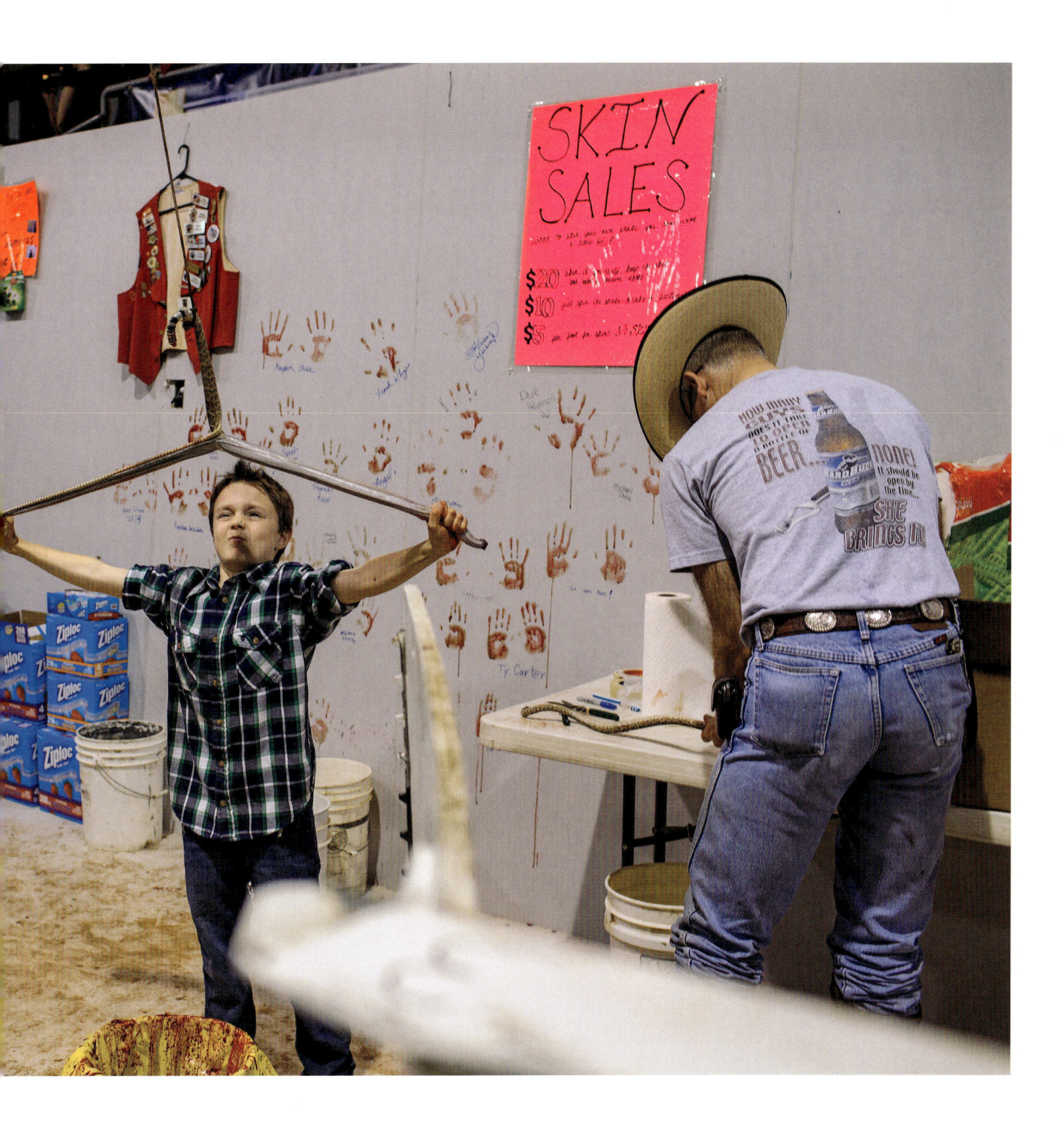

$20
$10
$5

158

159

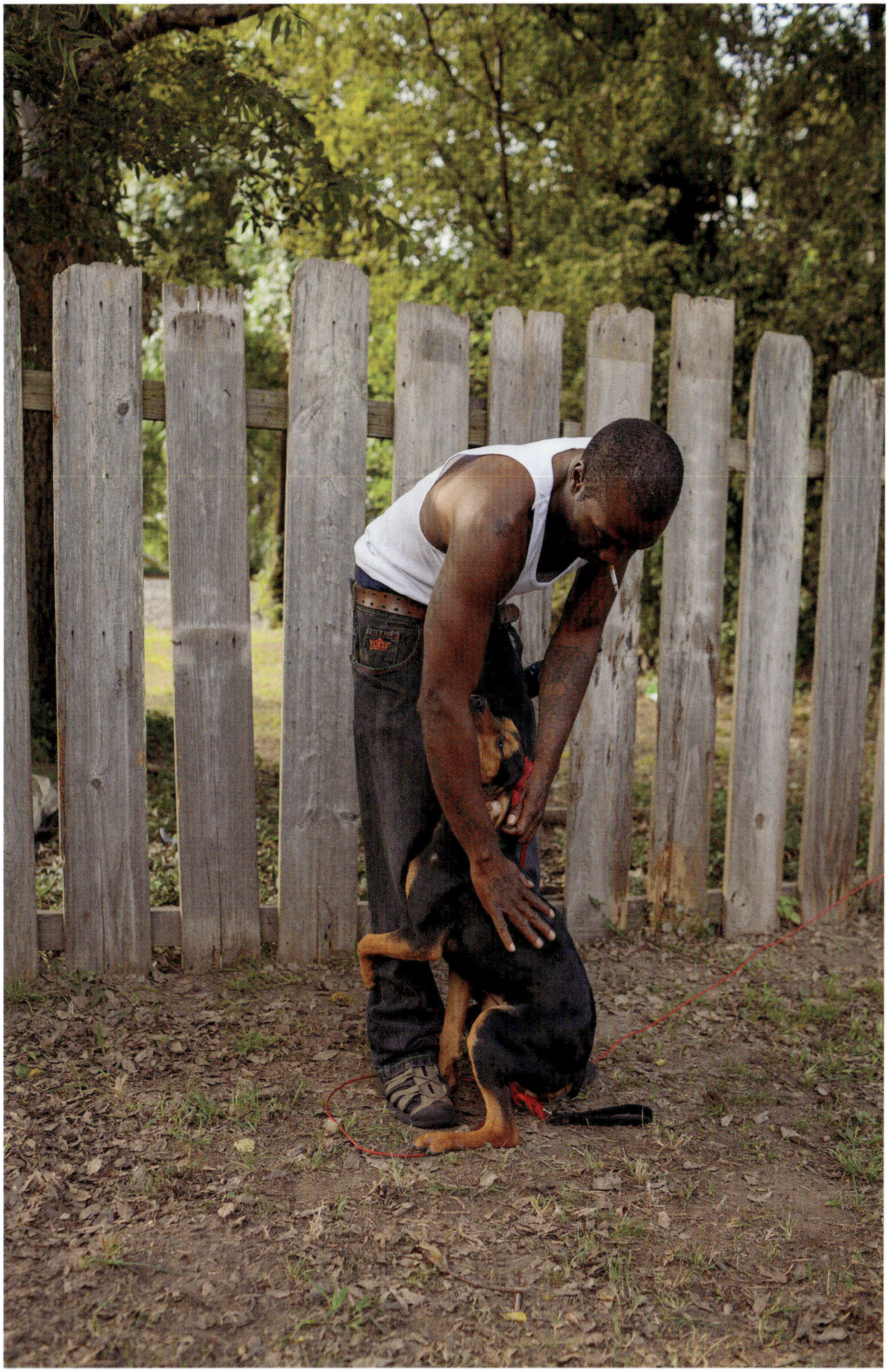

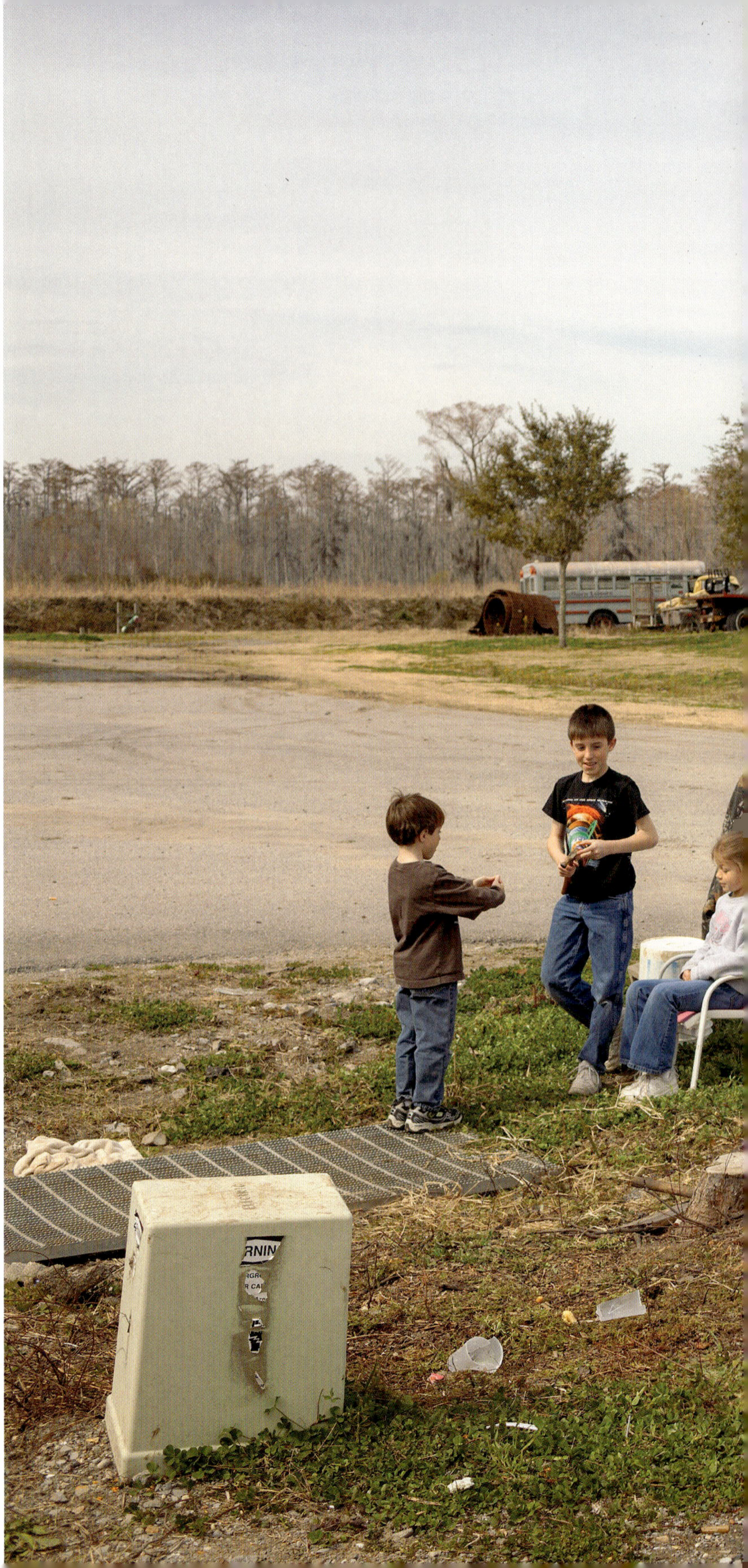

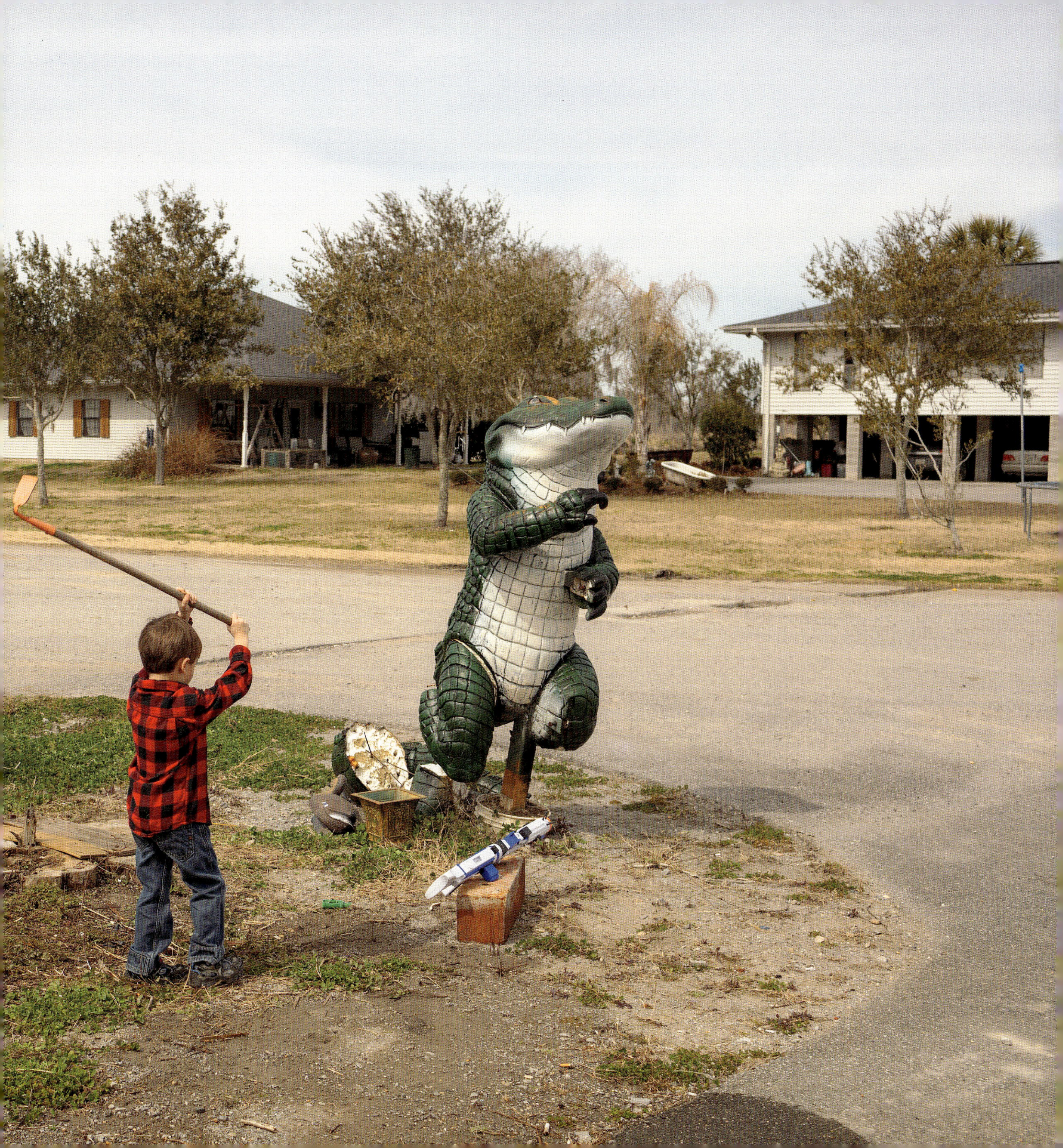

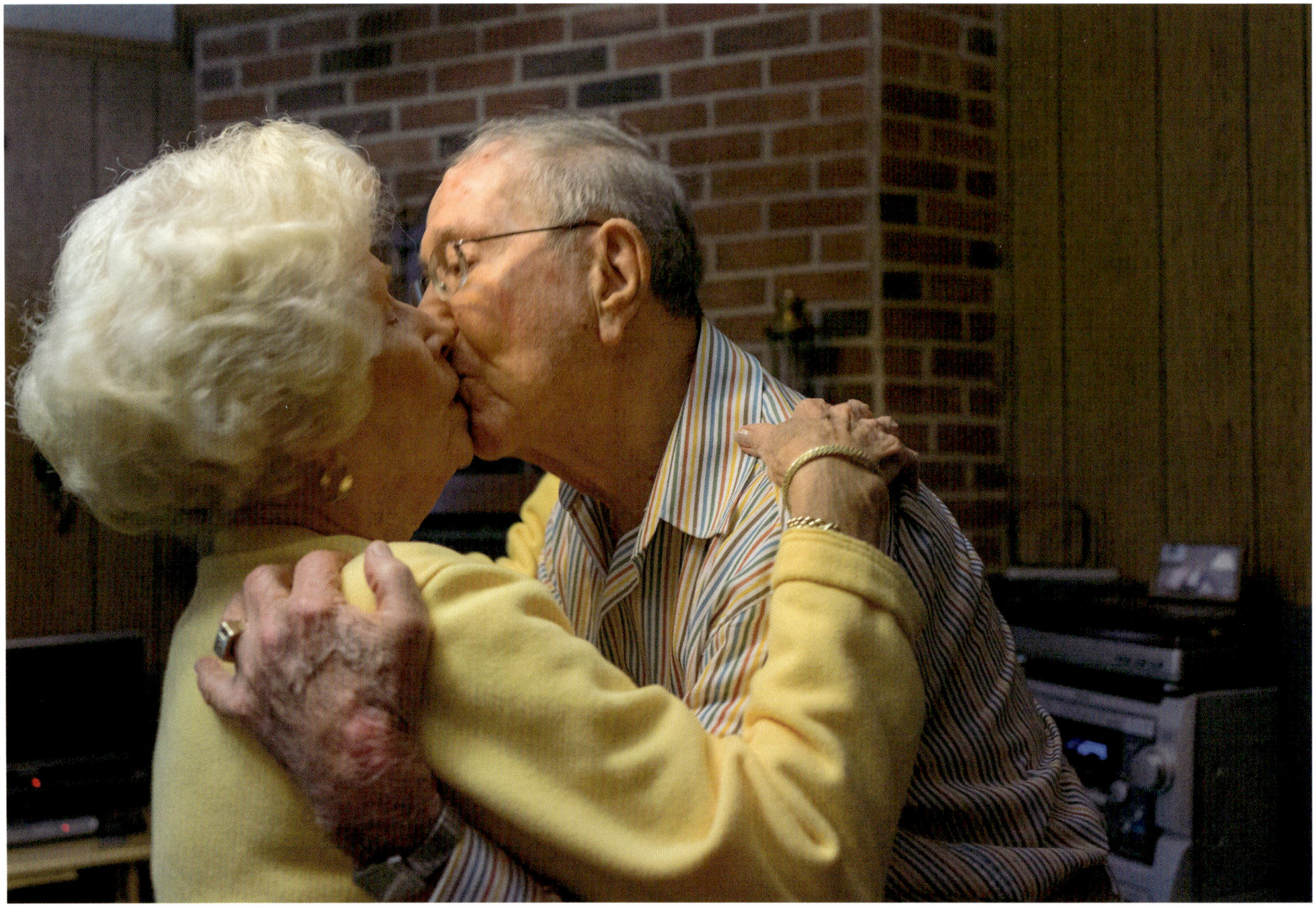

165

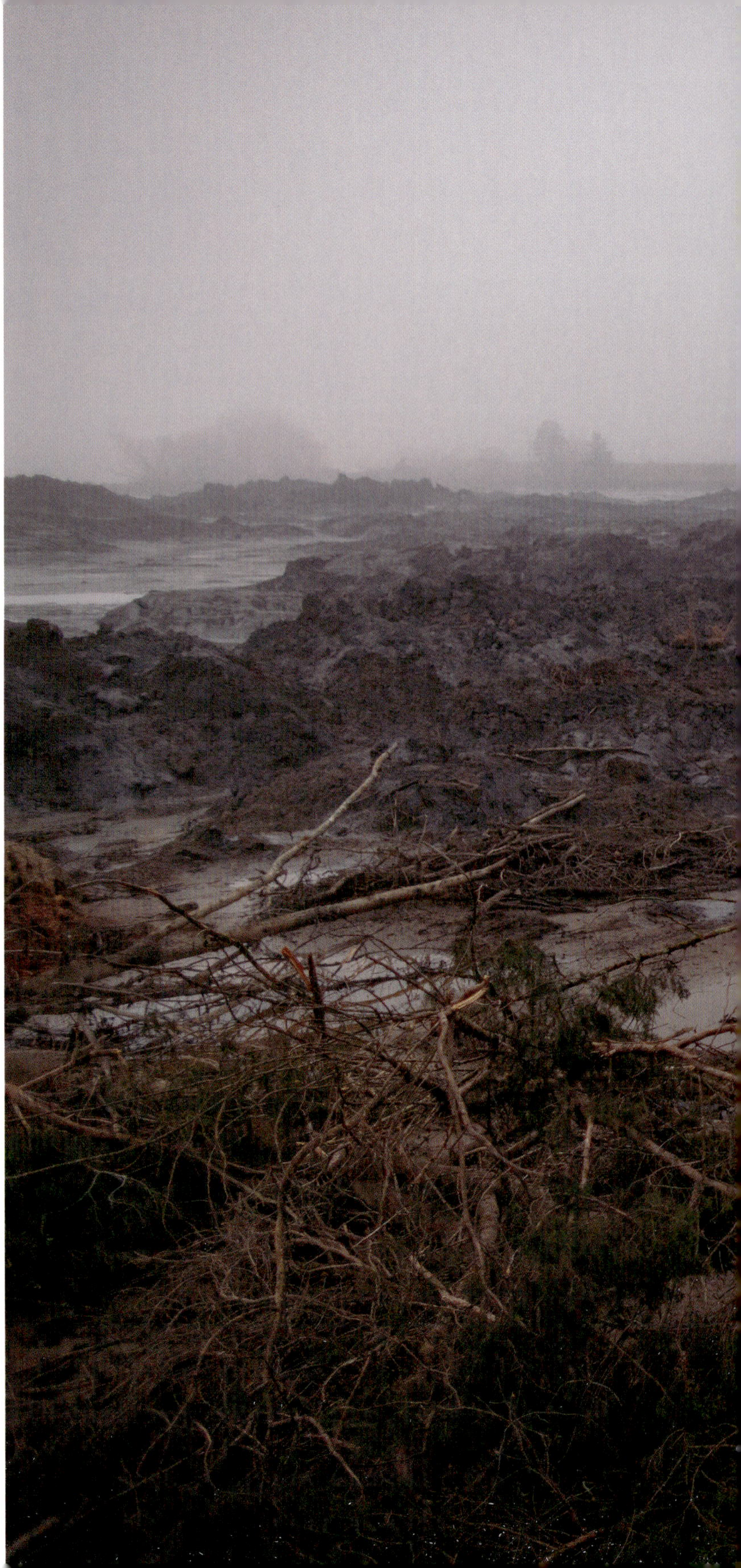

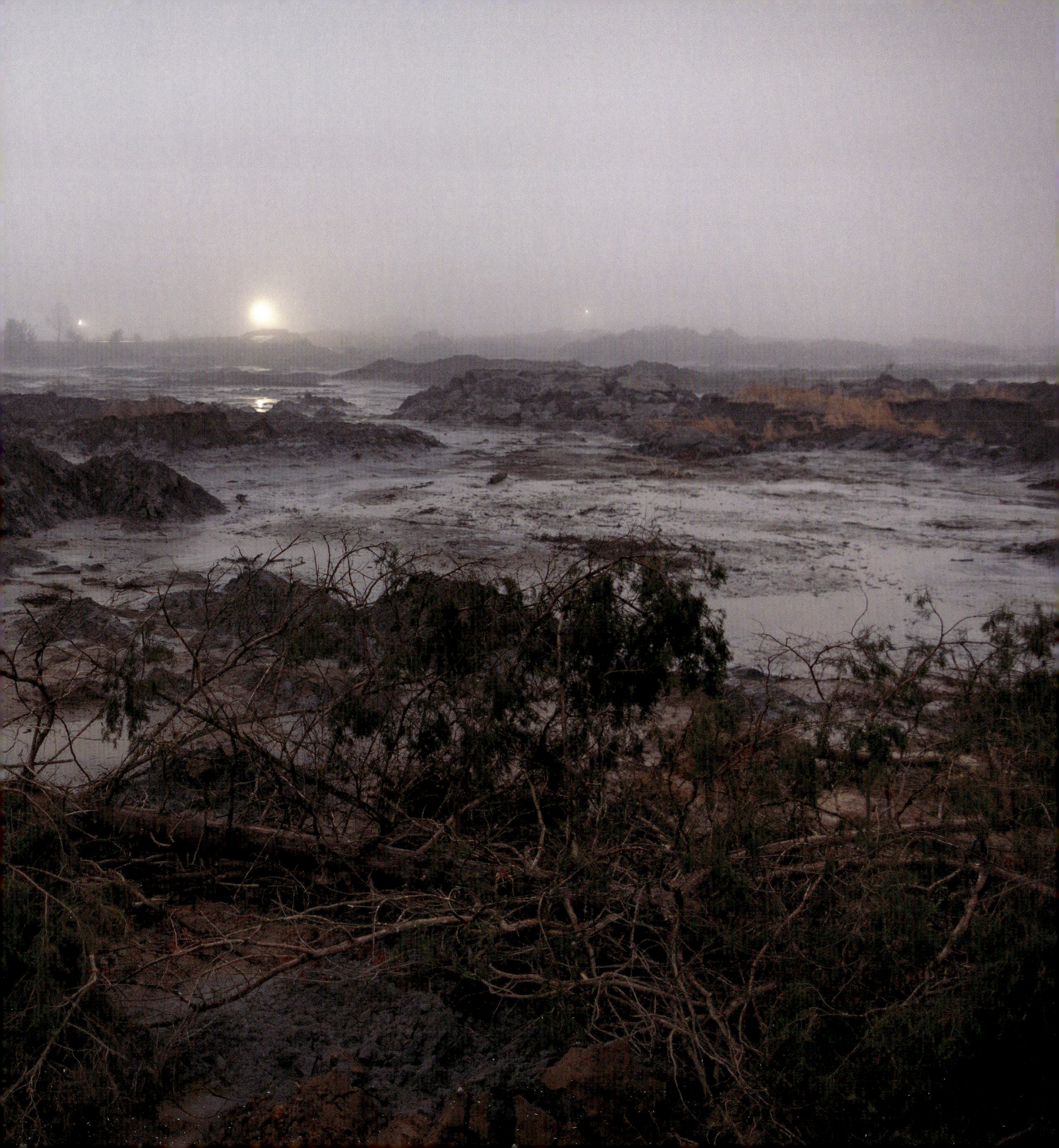

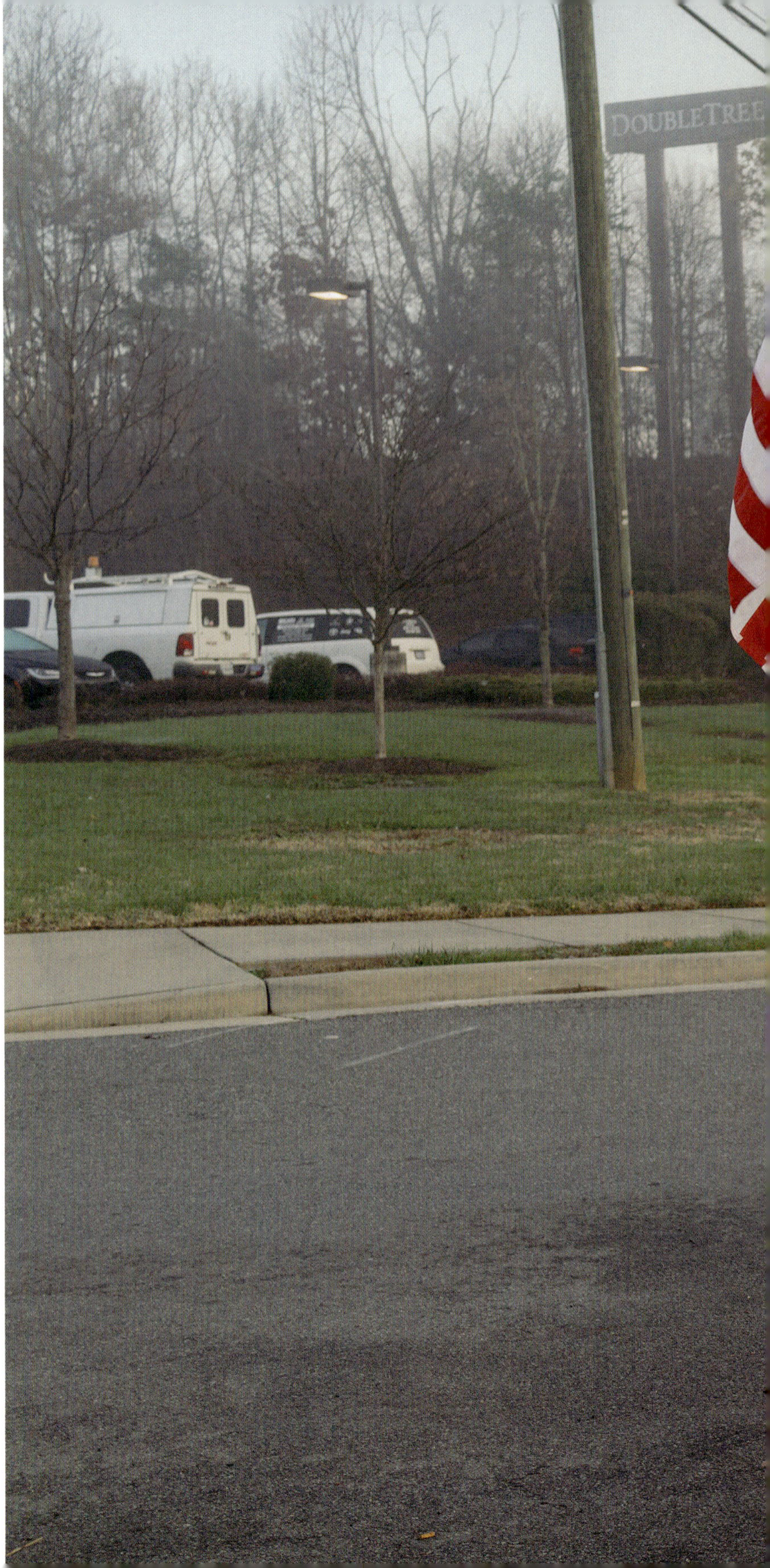
DOUBLETREE

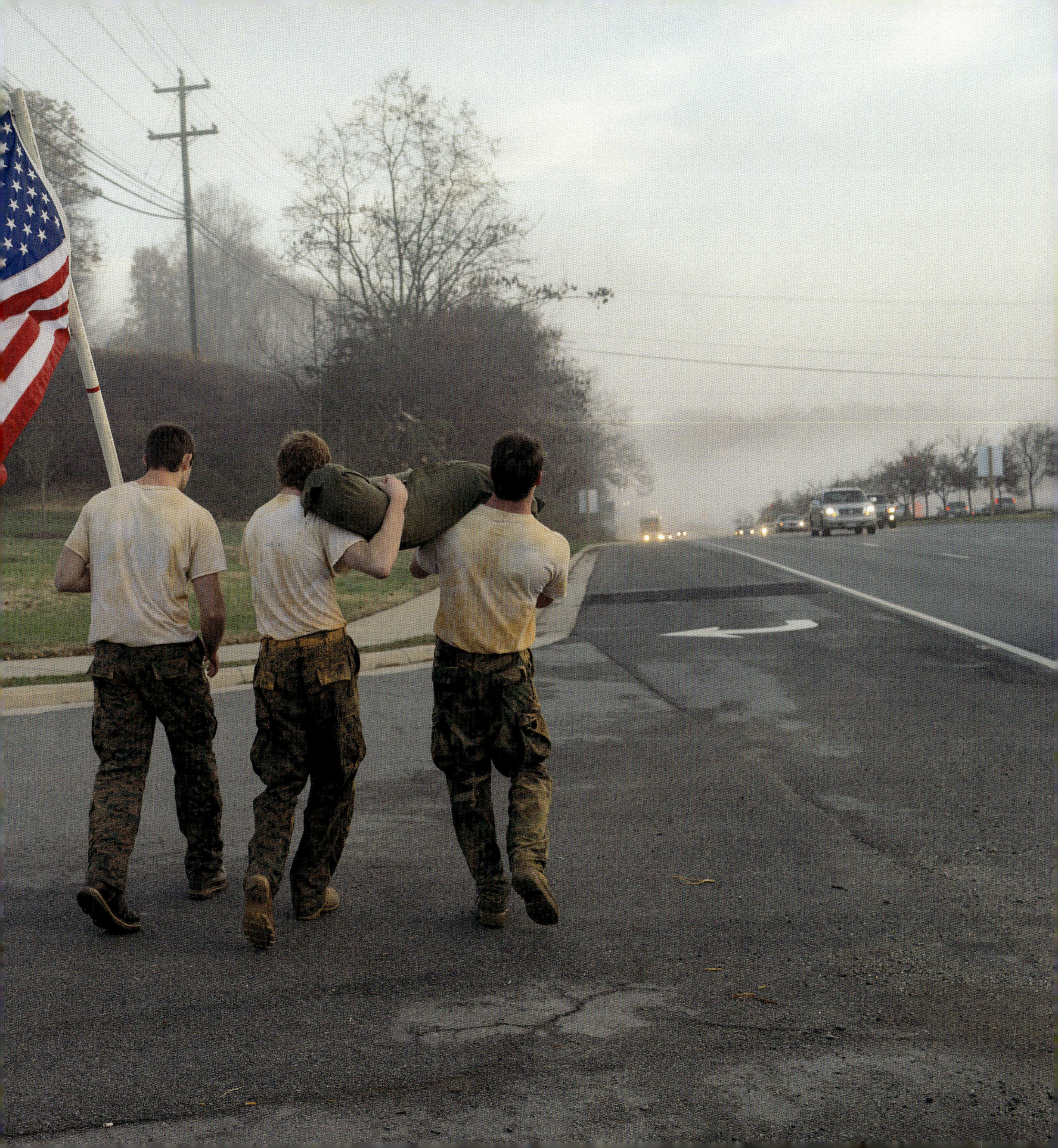

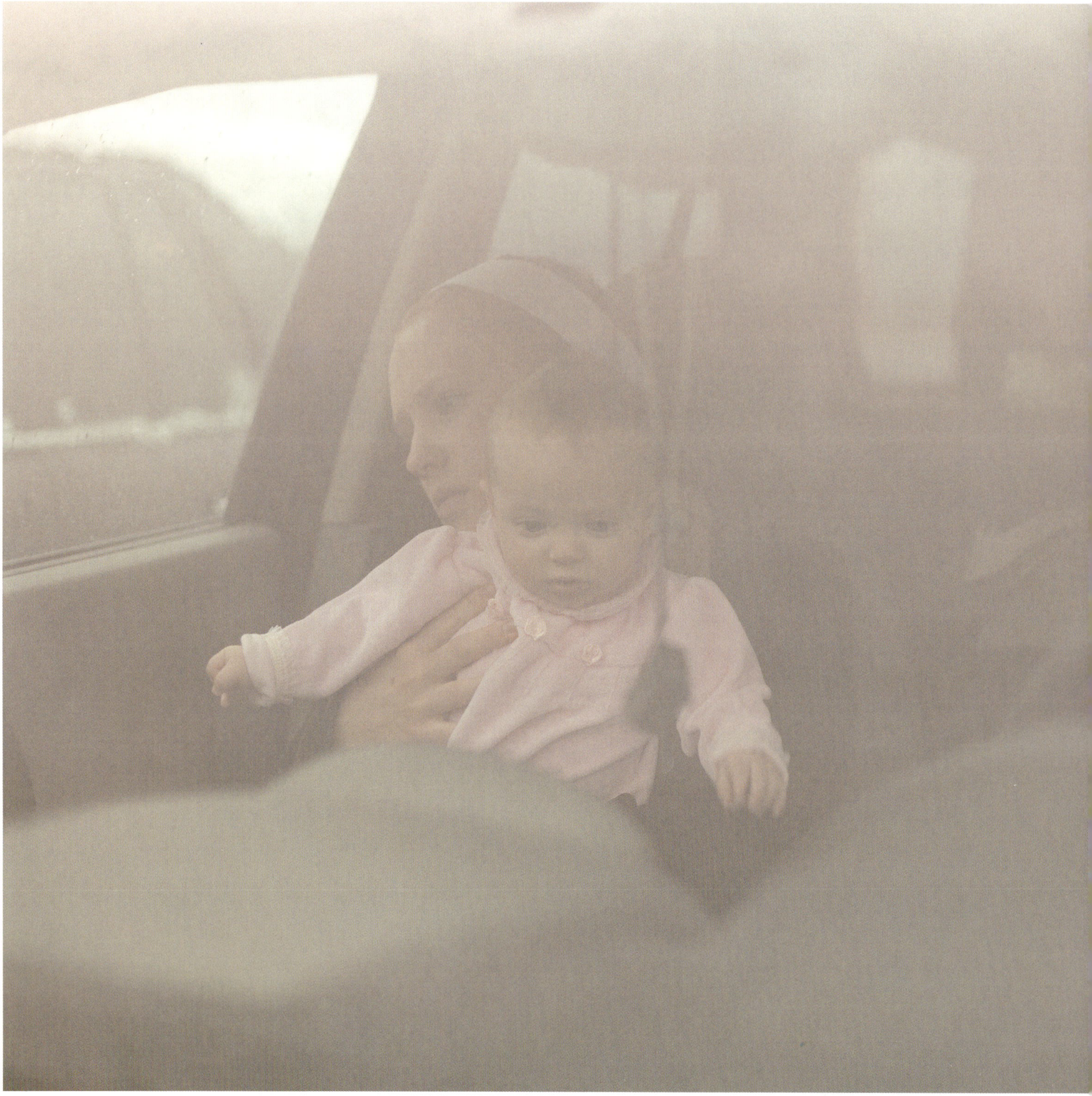

It is 2024 in America. I am 37 years old.

Through the course of making these photographs, my relationship to America and the medium of photography has grown heavier. What was once a creeping feeling, a gnawing worry, has now been made fully visible. My country is broken, and I fear it may be beyond repair. If you still believe the myth, you aren't paying attention.

The America of these photographs is gone, replaced by something darker, more paranoid, more self-destructive. For many it has always been a difficult and unjust land. When I look at these images, I think about how quickly time passes, how soon we will all be gone from this earth. And life will go on, in all its beauty, all its terribleness. I think about how heavy it feels to move through this world, but how light my efforts are when made tangible in the form of photographs. They are light as air. Like smoke. Unable to change a damn thing.

Despite my predisposition towards despair, I hope that America's arc can drift towards peace, justice, equity, and sustainability. While the photographs are inextricable from how I feel, they are meant to be about something more—a search for a shared humanity, an intimacy with strangers, the desire for an expanded empathy.

*—Matt Eich, Charlottesville, Virginia, May 2024*

# Images

08  **Untitled**, Belle, West Virginia, 2017

10  **At the club**, Greenwood, Mississippi, 2015

12  **Neighbors**, Norfolk, Virginia, 2014

14  **Paul's chickens**, Ivor, Virginia, 2010

16  **Calling the hounds**, Alabama, 2012

19  **Punxsutawney Phil**, Punxsutawney, Pennsylvania, 2012

21  **Untitled**, New York, New York, 2014

23  **Boys catching snakes**, Thermopolis, Wyoming, 2012

25  **After Hurricane Gustav**, Louisiana, 2008

27  **Children visiting their mothers in prison for Mother's Day**, California, 2006

28  **Untitled (Plumbing)**, Tangier Island, Virginia, 2017

31  **Man throwing Holi powder on Lee statue**, Charlottesville, Virginia, 2017

33  **Untitled (Cross)**, Tangier Island, Virginia, 2018

34  **Sunrise**, Seneca Rocks, West Virginia, 2015

35  **Couples at sunset**, Santa Barbara, California, 2014

37  **Couple sleeping on the subway**, New York, New York, 2014

38  **Untitled (caged bird)**, Tangier Island, Virginia, 2018

41  **Queshawn**, Richmond, Virginia, 2018

43  **Untitled (field burning)**, Mississippi, 2014

44  **Untitled (ice)**, Palmer, Alaska, 2017

45  **Untitled**, Charlottesville, Virginia, 2017

46  **ZayMyra and Whitney**, Richmond, Virginia, 2018

48  **Friends searching trash for a lost phone**, Herndon, Virginia, 2011

50  **Marlin (Kentucky Derby)**, Louisville, Kentucky, 2014

52  **Untitled (Parking)**, Louisville, Kentucky, 2014

54  **Haircut**, Greenwood, Mississippi, 2014

56  **Untitled (art world)**, New York, New York, 2014

58  **Double-tap**, near Shell Island, Louisiana, 2009

61  **Untitled**, Rapid City, South Dakota, 2014

63  **Joel Salatin with pigs**, Swoope, Virginia, 2011

64  **Papaw's 89th birthday**, Winston-Salem, North Carolina, 2011

66  **Untitled (kitchen)**, Portland, Oregon, 2007

69  **Madelyn with the stomach flu**, Charlottesville, Virginia, 2018

70  **Untitled (piano by the sea)**, Bodega Bay, California, 2014

72  **Madeline O'Dell, 102, and her daughter, Jean**, Chauncey, Ohio, 2012
74  **Mermaids and turtles**, Weeki Wachee, Florida, 2009
77  **Free**, North Carolina, 2015
79  **Untitled (by the water)**, Fairhope, Alabama, 2009
81  **Untitled (Mardi Gras)**, Mamou, Louisiana, 2010
83  **Hitchhiker**, between Virginia and Tennessee, 2014
85  **Boys riding in the back**, between Atlanta, Georgia and Norfolk, Virginia, 2011
87  **Untitled (sunsets on dirt roads)**, Chugwater, Wyoming, 2011
88  **Student gun owner**, Athens, Ohio, 2008
89  **Untitled (Stop bullets)**, Ohio, 2015
91  **Madelyn watches the eclipse**, Charlottesville, Virginia, 2017
92  **After the tornado**, Joplin, Missouri, 2011
94  **Quinceañera**, Dalton, Georgia, 2011
95  **90 Grados**, Manassas, Virginia, 2016
96  **Megachurch**, Birmingham, Alabama, 2015
98  **Untitled (Trump's Inauguration)**, Washington, D.C., 2017
100  **Country concert**, Bristol, Tennessee, 2016
103  **Untitled**, Mamou, Louisiana, 2009
104  **Naturalization Ceremony at Monticello**, Charlottesville, Virginia, 2018
106  **Alt-Right Soldiers**, Charlottesville, Virginia, 2017
108  **United States Capitol Building**, Washington, D.C., 2011
110  **Untitled (Confederate Flags)**, Richmond, Virginia, 2013
112  **Untitled (dead dog stuck under fence)**, West Virginia, 2011
114  **Groundhog Day**, Punxsutawney, Pennsylvania, 2012
116  **Mons Venus**, Tampa, Florida, 2009
119  **Untitled (3am train from New York Penn Station)**, New York, New York, 2014
120  **Dusk**, Ashland, Pennsylvania, 2012
122  **Town Foods**, Mamou, Louisiana, 2010
124  **Untitled**, New York, New York, 2013
125  **Untitled (Aftermath)**, Joplin, Missouri, 2011
126  **Baby in a bank**, Chugwater, Wyoming, 2011
128  **Swamp logging**, Windsor, North Carolina, 2009
130  **Untitled (Amazing Grace)**, Joplin, Missouri, 2011
133  **Prayer over breakfast before church**, Trussville, Alabama, 2015

## Images (continued)

134  **Fishing**, Blounts Creek, North Carolina, 2017
136  **Lunch break**, New York, New York, 2014
138  **Untitled (church service)**, Portland, Oregon, 2007
139  **Fourth of July**, Washington, D.C., 2008
140  **Knob Creek Machine Gun Shoot**, Knob Creek, Kentucky, 2011
142  **Untitled (flock of birds)**, Alabama, 2012
145  **Lovers on a park bench**, New York, New York, 2018
147  **Untitled (Parking #2)**, Louisville, Kentucky, 2014
148  **Halloween**, Tangier Island, Virginia, 2017
150  **Danny's Drive-In**, Ashland, Pennsylvania, 2012
153  **Untitled (light rays through tree)**, Washington, D.C., 2008
154  **Arrests after the murder of Michael Brown**, Ferguson, Missouri, 2014
155  **After the Battle at Bristol**, Bristol, Tennessee, 2016
156  **Skinning snakes**, Sweetwater, Texas, 2013
158  **Cat in fishing net**, Tangier Island, Virginia, 2010
159  **Chad Oba**, Union Hill, Virginia, 2018
161  **Winky with dog**, Greenwood, Mississippi, 2011
162  **Daneco Alligator Farm**, Houma, Louisiana, 2010
164  **Papaw kissing Anne**, Winston-Salem, North Carolina, 2014
165  **Untitled (Beach lovers)**, San Diego, California, 2016
166  **TVA Coal Ash Disaster**, Kingston, Tennessee, 2009
168  **Untitled**, Charlottesville, Virginia, 2015
170  **Maddie and Melissa in the car**, Athens, Ohio, 2008

# Acknowledgments

To Robert Frank and Eugene Richards for the gift of their eyes on this troubled land.

My deep and sincere gratitude to the friends and colleagues who have shaped, informed, and influenced my work and my life, including Rich-Joseph Facun, Kevin Martin, Amanda Lucier, Ross Taylor, Preston Gannaway, Nicole Frugé, Morgan Ashcom, Dustin Franz, Andy Spear, Pete Kiehart, Peter Hoffmann, Annie Flanagan, Kate Linthicum, Sol Neelman, Michael Rubenstein, Melissa Lyttle, Sarah Rice, Gina Martin, Noah Devereaux, Noah Rabinowitz, Ross Mantle, Leo Kim, Tyler Strickland, John Tully, Jenia Fridlyand, Aaron Hardin, Nate Grann, Pat Jarrett, Eliot Dudik, Jared Ragland, Lisa Elmaleh, Victor Blue, Bryan Derballa, Trent Davis Bailey, Tim Hussin, Peter McCollough, Ash Adams, Brian Adams, Tim Gruber, Christian Hansen, Peter van Agtmael, Philip Scott Andrews, Philip Montgomery, Justin Maxon, Mustafah Abdulaziz, Brandon Thibodeaux, Mark Peterson, Greta Pratt, Doug Van Gundy, Christopher Rauschenberg, Jennifer DeCarlo, and more folks than I can fit into these pages.

To the Sellers family, Goins family, Williams family, Wilson family, and everyone else who accepted me, took me in, and allowed me to make their picture over these many years. Thank you for seeing me, and for allowing me to see you.

To the editors who commissioned me to see this country over the years: Michael Wichita, Paul Moakley, Vaughn Wallace, Thea Traff, Marisa Schwartz-Taylor, Alison Unterreiner, Morrigan McCarthy, Matt Nighswander, Brent Murray, Mark Murrmann, Parker Eshelman, Justin O'Neill, Jim Surber, Barbara Stauss, Nicole Werbeck, Hannah McCaughey, Madeline Kelty, Michelle Molloy, Myles Little, Karen Frank, and anyone else that I have neglected to list here. Thanks for believing in me, and helping to support this work and my family.

To the Aevum and LUCEO crews: Chris Cappy, Yoon Byun, Elyse Butler, Matt Mallams, Andrew Henderson, David Walter Banks, Kendrick Brinson, Tim Lytvinenko, Kevin German, Daryl Peveto, and Matt Slaby. Thank you for your comradery in the early years.

Thank you to David Kasnic, Ian Bates, Steven Turville, Sam Owens, Roxi Pop, Clare Stimpson, Evie Metz, Alex Leck, Zack Wajsgras, Hadley Chittum, and Jack Fox for your friendship, your help in the studio, on assignments, and for generally being awesome.

To Mike and Deb Pang Davis for being part of this from the beginning. Mike, thank you for teaching me to begin to recognize my own pictures in the noise. This selection of images would not have taken shape without your guidance.

To my professors at Ohio University for setting me on a path: Stan Alost, Marcy Nighswander, Bruce Strong, Chad Stevens, and Terry Eiler, and to those at Hartford Art School for challenging me to expand my voice: Robert Lyons, Jörg Colberg, Michael Vahrenwald, Mary Frey, and the visiting faculty.

To my brilliant colleagues at Corcoran School of the Arts & Design at the George Washington University: Lauren Onkey, Dean Kessmann, Susan Sterner, Allyson Vieira, Michele Carlson, Marc Choi, Astrid Riecken, Michelle Frankfurter, Chan Chao, Caroline Casey, Kaitlin Jencso, and to my wonderful and dedicated students.

## Acknowledgements (continued)

Thank you to Ada Limón for the power and clarity of your words - they continue to comfort me. Thanks to Jesse Feinman for your help with the design and general insights, and to Allison Beondé for help with copy editing. Enormous thanks to Reto Caduff of Sturm & Drang for believing in this work for so long, and for patiently helping me bring it into the world, one piece at a time.

To my parents, David and Suzanne; my siblings, Hannah, Sarah, and Peter; brothers-in-law, Kenny and Chris; and to Amelie.

My eternal love and gratitude go to my wife, Melissa, and daughters, Madelyn and Meira, for their enduring love and patience. None of this would exist without you.

We, the Free
The Invisible Yoke Vol. IV

ISBN 978-3-906822-55-6

First Edition of 1,000 copies

© 2024 STURM & DRANG Publishers
All photographs © 2005 - 2024 MATT EICH
All rights reserved.

Ada Limón, "A New National Anthem" from The Carrying
Copyright © 2018 by Ada Limón
Reprinted with the permission of The Permissions Company LLC
on behalf of Milkweed Editions, milkweed.org.

DESIGN CONCEPT: Deborah Pang Davis
DESIGN: Jesse Feinman
PHOTO EDITOR: Mike Davis
SEQUENCE: Matt Eich and Reto Caduff
PRE-PRESS: John Wesley Mannion
COPY EDITOR: Allison Beondé
PRINTED in Germany by Wanderer Druck

DISTRIBUTED by Idea Books (NL) and Public Knowledge Books (UK)

No part of this book may be reproduced, altered, trimmed, laminated, mounted, or combined with any text or image to produce any form of derivative work. Nor may any part of this book be transmitted in any form or by any means, electronic or mechanical, including photocopying or recording, or by any information storage and retrieval system, without permission in writing from the publisher.

sturmanddrang.net
matteichphoto.com